PROJECT
WEBPAGES

A Collection of 180 Webpages
for People I May or May Not Know

by
Austin James Robinson & Co.

To everyone who was involved in this process over the past 2 years. I'm sorry it took so long.

CONTENTS

CREDITS

I would like to credit many people who made this project a reality. What started out as a joking status on Facebook turned into this book's prequel 'Project Letters' (2017), which led to what you are reading right now: 'Project Webpages'. More than 180 people made this possible. Of especially high importance is Lauren Myracle, whose 'TTYL' book series (2004) inspired the aesthetic of the webpages. I would also like to thank Christopher Sullivan and Tyler Corley, the former who designed the original book cover before I redesigned and adapted it for this sequel (also thanks, Adobe!), and the latter who has been there since day 1 of my web development journey. Tyler Durden and Ryan Mullowney also inspire me to continue my web development journey every day, while Connor Gleim helps me make great design decisions. This project's design and accompanying website could not have been realized without y'all!

Thank you.

FOREWORD
by KENETTE MANALO

Austin Robinson, a friend and colleague of mine, asked me to write a foreword for this project and compilation. At the time, I wasn't familiar with 'Project Letters' or 'Project Webpages' until he shared them with me. We became acquainted with one another in university during undergrad, but became increasingly closer years afterwards.

I thought about - and I still think about - how friendships and relationships change and evolve throughout the years, more specifically post-university friendships that solidify during shared hardships of finding one's identity and passion through work and adulthood. I find that the job search experience can be an incredibly bonding one, as the journey can be a rollercoaster. It reminds me how important it is to lean on others not only during times of joy, but also during times of distress. And that's exactly what Austin provides for me.

Based on the way I evaluate friendships and life, I can view others and the opportunities they present as ROIs (Return On Investments). I believe Austin helps to challenge these thoughts, especially after reading the manuscript for 'Project Webpages'. I also know Austin as one to engage with his respective communities, whether it be UT networks or strangers on social media. He leverages the internet to foster connections that can feel so deep and personal, no matter how far away the person is. To me, these qualities are beyond admirable.

This book emphasizes the importance of connection, which arrives at a time that is unique and strange. A pandemic that results in so much loss and pain needs a little light, no matter how bright. This project commemorates the idea that something is never too late. I've lost friends this year, regained some of those friends, and found that friendships can outgrow one another. I realized that friendships and relationships can wither from a lack of appreciation and validation from the participants. I think about relationships that are so grand - Prince Charles and Princess Diana, for example - that they lack the foundation of being heard and valued. Ultimately, people want to be understood and heard.

Austin's project captures the essence of being understood and heard when he asks you, simply, what your favorite color is or to recite your fondest memory. Sometimes we want to be asked what our third favorite Australian animal is. Sometimes we don't vocalize who we are or what we value enough. There's so much to learn about someone, and it makes me wonder how much someone is dying to share. How can we support one another? I admire this project to the point that I wish I was involved sooner than now. At the same time, I know I will be involved in his next friendship project.

'Project Webpages' also inspires creativity through journey and color motifs. Austin expresses how friendships and relationships are a two-way street, and asks the participants to write back and facilitate the shared appreciation they have with him. I'm honored to be reminded of that appreciation with others in my own life. Not only do I value mine and Austin's friendship and closeness together, I'm also in awe of his aura and the impact his projects create. I believe that, at the heart, this two-and-a-half year project inspires thought, community, and love at any level of friendship.

I hope you enjoy 'Project Webpages' as much as I did.

- Kenette Ray Manalo
Friend & Colleague to Austin Robinson

A

Before I get into this book, let me tell you about its predecessor: 'Project Letters'. Back in 2017, I jokingly posted a status with the sole intention of poking fun at individuals who go on the web and post things like "LMS for a TBH!" or whatever. In case you didn't understand what I just said, essentially I asked people to 'like' or 'react' to a status of mine on Facebook for a personalized letter. Here, I'll just show you:

 Austin James Robinson
April 12 · 🌐 ▾

haha like this status and I'll write a 250-word double-spaced MLA-cited Microsoft Word 2010 document about what I like about you and email it to you

👍 Like　　💬 Comment　　➡ Share

 Varun Adiga, ▮▮▮▮▮▮ and 255 others

After posting that, I proceeded to write a 254-page book that held every single letter I wrote to the people who 'liked' it. Although you don't need to read 'Project

Letters' to understand what I'm doing in this book, you can find it on any major online bookstore.

When the anniversary of 'Project Letters' came around in April of 2018, I decided I would start the journey to create its spiritual successor. Once again, I implored my friends and acquaintances on Facebook to 'like' or 'react' to my status. However this time, instead of a simple letter, I went all in: I vowed to create a single personalized webpage for each person.

Austin J. Robinson
April 19, 2018 ·

haha like this status and I'll create a unique & personalized web page on my website that is passcode protected (only you and I will know) and tell you what I like about you TBH

👍😮😊 181   36 Comments

👍 Like   💬 Comment   ↪ Share

The original plan was to tack on 180 webpages to my pre-built WIX website, make them uniquely passcode protected, and send them individually to each person. Those were the simple days. I sent a Facebook message to each individual asking their favorite color, their favorite memory with me, and pictures they may have of the two of us together. I even logged all of this information and had the entire project planned out. *I completed 'Project Letters' in 1 month, so how hard could this be?* I naively thought to myself. Just like lightning, a stroke of genius never strikes twice. I quickly discovered that a website building service can only hold so many individual pages before lagging - plus, I was moving to Canada less than a month after promising these webpages. One thing led to another, and suddenly I had moved from Texas to Canada back to Texas to Portland all within the span of 4 months. I found a job on Craigslist in Portland - a place I had never visited before and could not locate on a map - and immediately packed my bags. Turns out, it was a pretty illegitimate business (hence the presence of Craigslist), and I ended up living in what I'm calling a "Punk House" with several individuals who live fast and you know the rest.

Anyway, all of that to say: I did not complete 'Project Webpages' in 2018. Or 2019. And this is barely coming to you in 2020. I'm sure a good portion of the individuals who originally 'liked' my Facebook status no longer consider me a friend. I know for a fact a good one or two hate me. (That's not going to stop me from making them a webpage though!) And a majority of the people I consider very close in my life now didn't know about my existence when I made the original Facebook post - so it honestly feels weird creating a friendship appreciation novel without including them. Alas, I am fooling myself into thinking the year is 2018 and that I work at a skating rink with all the time in the world again. Hey, it beats Coronavirus.

Before I showcase the wonderful webpages, I have some ground rules I need you to know in order to fully understand this book:

> - I no longer use WIX as a website builder. In fact, I picked up web development back in spring

of 2019 to have more creative freedom over projects such as this.

- My Facebook status originally stated the webpages would be uniquely and individually passcode protected. That would require a lot more work, so I've decided to just change everyone's name. None of the last names in this book or on the website are real.

- If you bought the physical copy of this book, the webpages will be in black and white. That's because this book is only $10 in black and white, but $25 in color. Not even I would buy my own book for $25. If you want to see the website in the full spectrum of color (180 different shades!), go to www.projectweb.page.

- As I alluded to earlier, I originally wanted each webpage to be hyper-personalized, down to the individual's favorite color, memory, and pictures. This type of overextension is exactly why it has taken me 2.5 years to complete this project. The webpage template is uniform across webpages, sans color and content. The fact that I made them actual webpages and not just pages in a book makes me feel okay with this downgrade.

- I totally understand that the "webpages" look more like an IM chat room than a website. Just go with it.

- You'll notice a handwritten font at the end of each webpage. That's my handwriting! To make up for the fact that I didn't deliver my promise on time or as spectacular as I would have liked, I created my own font just for you. I would have written the entire webpage in my font, but then it would be super hard to read.

Hi! You liked my status about a TBH webpage! This is a continuation of the friendship project I completed last year: Project Letters. In order for me to create your unique passcode-protected webpage on my website, I have a couple questions you need to answer.

But first, what's your email address (or other form of communication you prefer)? I will send the questions over there and then we can get started.

It may take a couple months to complete this project because I have a lot of pages to make. xo

The Facebook message I sent to each person after they 'liked' my status.

Just like 'Project Letters', this project took me over 100 hours to complete. From messaging every single person to coding their webpage to creating my own font, etc., I can confidently say I logged well over 100 hours. It's funny because after I completed 'Project Letters', a lot of people said, "You must have a lot of time on your hands!" Now I'm writing the sequel in the age of the Coronavirus, so people are saying, "Oh yeah that makes sense." Regardless, the fact of the matter is: I posted the status, I committed to publicly admiring my friends, and I created these webpages. And on top of that, I wrote this book.

People have also asked me why I created not one, but TWO projects that take an incredible amount of time to complete and were developed from a joke. To that I say... actually, I'm just going to copy and paste how I answered a similar question in the first book:

Now, why did I do this? That is a valid question. What kind of person just decides to spend an exuberant amount of time writing nice words to friends (and, in some cases, strangers) on the web? And what compels that person to then create a book documenting the entire process? Well, let me tell you a little bit about my stance on friendship. Friends are the celebrities of my reality. I do not – nor have I really ever – worship conventional celebrities. I find the entire idea of idolizing people on a screen mildly interesting at best. When I was in high school, I got a t-shirt made that said my best friend's name on it. I did so because I really appreciated them at the time, I wanted to showcase that I love them, and I considered them a celebrity in my life. Since then, I have created at least a dozen more t-shirts filled with the names of best friends, family members, and even people who have just completely changed my life. It got to the point where I was choosing which 'name' t-shirt to wear based on how I wanted to feel that day. Did I want to do well on an exam and feel hella smart in my classes? I'd put on my 'Colten' t-shirt. Did I want to kick life in the face and own the world for the day? I'd put on my 'Kate' t-shirt. I had more than a dozen t-shirts to choose from, all with a completely different personality and energy that I could channel whenever I pleased.

Then I began to realize that people are what matter the most in my life. I have always valued friendship above all else. The wellness of another human being oftentimes takes precedence over everything in my life. A good friend once told me, "If I had to choose between studying for a last-minute exam or helping someone in a way that is substantial to their life, I will always choose the latter." I immediately made a shirt with their name on it. Philosophies such as these are what make life worth living to me. So over the course of reading these webpages, I want you to keep your friends and loved ones in mind.

Enjoy.

THE WEBPAGES

So here they are! The webpages. You will notice they are in alphabetical order by first name. As I mentioned earlier, the last names have been changed to give everyone anonymity. Each webpage was carefully crafted and personalized to showcase either the memories of friendship I had with the person or something about their character that I intensely appreciate. You'll notice that sometimes I didn't know someone well. I did not want to ignore their importance – albeit small – in my life, so they are included. A reminder that if you are reading the physical copy of this book, the webpages that follow will be in black and white because I wanted to make this book $10 and not $25. If you want to see the webpages in full color, please head to www.projectweb.page.

Friday, November 20th, 16:45

Aaron Smith,

If you're reading this, it's because you 'liked' a Facebook post I made back in 2018. I know it's been awhile, but I'm happy to present your very own webpage and my favorite memory with you!

My favorite memory with you is not only being part of Alpha Phi Omega with you, but also the fact that you are such a go-getter who takes leaps and isn't afraid of where you land. You also aren't afraid to have regrets - or maybe you just don't have any. Either way, it is inspiring and I'm grateful I got to learn that from you. I hope you're having the time of your life!

I cherish you and I want you to know our memories together hold a special place in my heart. You're included in the collective experiences that make me who I am today, and I am forever grateful.

— Austin Robinson

Send   Cancel

Friday, November 20th, 16:49

Adam Bennett,

If you're reading this, it's because you 'liked' a Facebook post I made back in 2018. I know it's been awhile, but I'm happy to present your very own webpage and my favorite memory with you!

My favorite memory with you is when I visited you in Chicago and got to see into the world of cross-dressing and screamo bands that help you express your identity and emotions. I'm glad we got to share many secrets over drinks that night. That was pretty kick-ass. I'm also obsessed with your zines and artwork, and can't wait to see where your artistic visions take you!

I cherish you and I want you to know our memories together hold a special place in my heart. You're included in the collective experiences that make me who I am today, and I am forever grateful.

— Austin Robinson

Send   Cancel

Friday, November 20th, 16:54

Adam Williams,

If you're reading this, it's because you 'liked' a Facebook post I made back in 2018. I know it's been awhile, but I'm happy to present your very own webpage and my favorite memory with you!

My favorite memory with you is when we got to know each other at HOBY and then you came to me with questions about the University of Texas at Austin, and eventually about running for various Student Government positions. I feel a kinship with the few people who end up running for office at UT. You're such a go-getter, and I know we see ourselves in each other!

I cherish you and I want you to know our memories together hold a special place in my heart. You're included in the collective experiences that make me who I am today, and I am forever grateful.

— Austin Robinson

 Send   Cancel

Friday, November 20th, 16:59

Adam Hall,

If you're reading this, it's because you 'liked' a Facebook post I made back in 2018. I know it's been awhile, but I'm happy to present your very own webpage and my favorite memory with you!

My favorite memory with you is when we had a huge discussion surrounding the philosophy of ethics and the law behind recording people without their knowledge (which is legal in Texas for some reason!). I believe you opened up my eyes with your stance, and helped me grow as a person who now thinks critically about the ethics of human interactions!

I cherish you and I want you to know our memories together hold a special place in my heart. You're included in the collective experiences that make me who I am today, and I am forever grateful.

— Austin Robinson

Send   Cancel

Friday, November 20th, 17:29

Afshan Young,

If you're reading this, it's because you 'liked' a Facebook post I made back in 2018. I know it's been awhile, but I'm happy to present your very own webpage and my favorite memory with you!

My favorite memory with you is when we FaceTime'd shortly after I moved to Portland. For some reason, I vividly remember that call. I was in Northeast Portland and was walking by an AT&T store (not sponsored). Of course we had some great memories while we were in university and similar organizations together, but that FaceTime always stands out to me!

I cherish you and I want you to know our memories together hold a special place in my heart. You're included in the collective experiences that make me who I am today, and I am forever grateful.

— Austin Robinson

Send   Cancel

Friday, November 20th, 17:32

Ahmed Morris,

If you're reading this, it's because you 'liked' a Facebook post I made back in 2018. I know it's been awhile, but I'm happy to present your very own webpage and my favorite memory with you!

My favorite memory with you is when you showed the entire Circle K club the Nicki Minaj music video that you totally starred in! Absolutely NO ONE was expecting that and I think we will all respect you forever. I also love contributing to your cause when you run for the Susan G. Komen Breast Cancer Awareness foundation. I'll financially support it for as long as I can!

I cherish you and I want you to know our memories together hold a special place in my heart. You're included in the collective experiences that make me who I am today, and I am forever grateful.

— Austin Robinson

Send   Cancel

Friday, November 20th, 17:35

Alandar Stewart,

If you're reading this, it's because you 'liked' a Facebook post I made back in 2018. I know it's been awhile, but I'm happy to present your very own webpage and my favorite memory with you!

My favorite memory with you is all of the hilarious tweets you consistently put out, as well as the total looks and adventures you have. I can't believe I know so many people who know you, but that we've never met before! And you introduced me to Gabe, who is an amazing human being. You're definitely at the top of the list when I start visiting Twitter people after quarantine!

I cherish you and I want you to know our memories together hold a special place in my heart. You're included in the collective experiences that make me who I am today, and I am forever grateful.

– Austin Robinson

Send   Cancel

Friday, November 20th, 17:38

Alden Zachary,

If you're reading this, it's because you 'liked' a Facebook post I made back in 2018. I know it's been awhile, but I'm happy to present your very own webpage and my favorite memory with you!

My favorite memory with you is all of the times we spent in the UT Austin Student Government and Senate lounge, and how entirely dedicated you are to politics and the lives of others that politics affects. You had such a passion for student life and you were such a go-getter, and I can see that carried on into your post-graduate life. I can't wait to see what you do!

I cherish you and I want you to know our memories together hold a special place in my heart. You're included in the collective experiences that make me who I am today, and I am forever grateful.

— Austin Robinson

Send   Cancel

Friday, November 20th, 17:40

Alex Jones,

If you're reading this, it's because you 'liked' a Facebook post I made back in 2018. I know it's been awhile, but I'm happy to present your very own webpage and my favorite memory with you!

First of all, I just want to apologize for the unfortunate name my name generator gave you. You don't deserve that! My favorite memory with you is the deep talks about relationships and gay culture at UT that we used to have. You were always passionate about supporting great causes at the university, in Austin, and in the US. You're definitely going to change the world!

I cherish you and I want you to know our memories together hold a special place in my heart. You're included in the collective experiences that make me who I am today, and I am forever grateful.

— Austin Robinson

Send   Cancel

Friday, November 20th, 17:45

Annecy Price,

If you're reading this, it's because you 'liked' a Facebook post I made back in 2018. I know it's been awhile, but I'm happy to present your very own webpage and my favorite memory with you!

We've never met, but I've watched your life unfold on Facebook and I just want to say that you're doing a great job at being a caring human being and taking care of yourself. Although we don't have any memories together, I hope that I get to meet you someday and have critical conversations with you about social problems that we experience and see in the world!

I cherish you and I want you to know our memories together hold a special place in my heart. You're included in the collective experiences that make me who I am today, and I am forever grateful.

– Austin Robinson

Send   Cancel

Friday, November 20th, 17:48

Austin Edgar,

If you're reading this, it's because you 'liked' a Facebook post I made back in 2018. I know it's been awhile, but I'm happy to present your very own webpage and my favorite memory with you!

My favorite memory with you is when you let me sneak into the carillon room at UT Austin and showed me all of the things you use to make the bell ring at the tower! It was such a cool and unique experience to have during my undergraduate years. It's great to follow your journey on social media and see that you're doing so well for yourself. Keep it up!

I cherish you and I want you to know our memories together hold a special place in my heart. You're included in the collective experiences that make me who I am today, and I am forever grateful.

— Austin Robinson

Send   Cancel

Friday, November 20th, 17:50

Austin Carnes,

If you're reading this, it's because you 'liked' a Facebook post I made back in 2018. I know it's been awhile, but I'm happy to present your very own webpage and my favorite memory with you!

My favorite memory with you is when we first met at HOBY in 2013. The very moment we met. You are one of my favorite human beings, so that moment was critical for the ones that followed and still follow to this day. You are impeccable. You are changing the world with your teaching and you are going after what makes you happy in an unknown place. I love you!

I cherish you and I want you to know our memories together hold a special place in my heart. You're included in the collective experiences that make me who I am today, and I am forever grateful.

— Austin Robinson

Send   Cancel

Friday, November 20th, 17:52

Austin Allens,

If you're reading this, it's because you 'liked' a Facebook post I made back in 2018. I know it's been awhile, but I'm happy to present your very own webpage and my favorite memory with you!

I truly have no idea who you are, but apparently we've been friends on Facebook for years. I know you went to UT with me and that you're really good friends with other people I know. Let's see, what I can say to a stranger... OH! I want to say that I really, really appreciate your first name. Thank you for deciding to have the same exact name as me. It's really brave of us!

I cherish you and I want you to know our memories together hold a special place in my heart. You're included in the collective experiences that make me who I am today, and I am forever grateful.

— Austin Robinson

Send   Cancel

Friday, November 20th, 20:39

Ben Rogers,

If you're reading this, it's because you 'liked' a Facebook post I made back in 2018. I know it's been awhile, but I'm happy to present your very own webpage and my favorite memory with you!

My favorite memory with you is when you made me Matzo Ball Soup in your Chicago apartment (my first time trying it!) and didn't mind when I was sick and still coming over every single day. I also loved pretending like I knew everything about Chemistry while you were literally getting your PhD in Chemistry. You made my time in Chicago so special!

I cherish you and I want you to know our memories together hold a special place in my heart. You're included in the collective experiences that make me who I am today, and I am forever grateful.

– Austin Robinson

 Send Cancel

Brandon Brown,

If you're reading this, it's because you 'liked' a Facebook post I made back in 2018. I know it's been awhile, but I'm happy to present your very own webpage and my favorite memory with you!

My favorite memory with you is when we would get to hang out during Alpha Phi Omega seminars. You and your crew at UNT were some of the most fun people to ever be around. Not to mention y'all repped my AUSTIN JAMES ROBINSON shirt pretty hard. I missing hanging out on the Denton Square with y'all! Also, it's pretty wild that I saw you at a Dallas night club that one time!

I cherish you and I want you to know our memories together hold a special place in my heart. You're included in the collective experiences that make me who I am today, and I am forever grateful.

– Austin Robinson

Send   Cancel

Friday, November 20th, 20:44

Bret Allen,

If you're reading this, it's because you 'liked' a Facebook post I made back in 2018. I know it's been awhile, but I'm happy to present your very own webpage and my favorite memory with you!

My favorite memory with you is actually two memories. The first is when we ate at that Ethiopian place in Austin, Texas and I tried injera bread for the first time. The second is when you let me spend the night and I accidentally spilled red wine on your couch because it was one of the first times I ever got drunk. I hope you left your job at Samsung and that you're happy now!

I cherish you and I want you to know our memories together hold a special place in my heart. You're included in the collective experiences that make me who I am today, and I am forever grateful.

— Austin Robinson

Send   Cancel

Friday, November 20th, 20:46

Brett King,

If you're reading this, it's because you 'liked' a Facebook post I made back in 2018. I know it's been awhile, but I'm happy to present your very own webpage and my favorite memory with you!

I remember reading your pretty popular comic strips in 8th grade. EIGHTH GRADE. It is wild that I would then go on to be your friend 8 years later. That is truly serendipitous. My favorite memory with you is when we got drinks at a bar in Tucson, Arizona and you asked me if I'd be willing to share a Comic Con merchant table with you. I still can't get over it all!

I cherish you and I want you to know our memories together hold a special place in my heart. You're included in the collective experiences that make me who I am today, and I am forever grateful.

– Austin Robinson

Send   Cancel

Friday, November 20th, 20:49

Brian Reed,

If you're reading this, it's because you 'liked' a Facebook post I made back in 2018. I know it's been awhile, but I'm happy to present your very own webpage and my favorite memory with you!

My favorite memory with you is when I saw you play with your bluegrass band at a UT Austin Student Government meeting. I truly had no idea that you were part of a bluegrass band until that moment and it made me have so much respect for you. I appreciate how much you did for Alpha Phi Omega and how much love you had for our university!

I cherish you and I want you to know our memories together hold a special place in my heart. You're included in the collective experiences that make me who I am today, and I am forever grateful.

— Austin Robinson

Send   Cancel

Friday, November 20th, 20:55

Brianna Sanchez,

If you're reading this, it's because you 'liked' a Facebook post I made back in 2018. I know it's been awhile, but I'm happy to present your very own webpage and my favorite memory with you!

My favorite memory with you is when we were together in Key Club and had such fun at conventions together! I know we haven't really talked since high school, but I always found it cool that you were from Wisconsin and would talk about it all the time, especially because not a lot of people in our hometown experience what's outside of it. I hope you're doing well!

I cherish you and I want you to know our memories together hold a special place in my heart. You're included in the collective experiences that make me who I am today, and I am forever grateful.

— Austin Robinson

Send   Cancel

Friday, November 20th, 20:57

Brittanie Ross,

If you're reading this, it's because you 'liked' a Facebook post I made back in 2018. I know it's been awhile, but I'm happy to present your very own webpage and my favorite memory with you!

My favorite memory with you is when we attended the HOBY Texas North conference together a couple of times and always had a ton of fun. I feel like you were one of the few volunteers there who actually understood me and that I could laugh with. There was a great connection there and I hope you're living your life making everyone around you laugh!

I cherish you and I want you to know our memories together hold a special place in my heart. You're included in the collective experiences that make me who I am today, and I am forever grateful.

— Austin Robinson

Send   Cancel

Friday, November 20th, 20:59

Brittany David,

If you're reading this, it's because you 'liked' a Facebook post I made back in 2018. I know it's been awhile, but I'm happy to present your very own webpage and my favorite memory with you!

My favorite memory with you is when we would hang out and just gossip about our mutual friend Will (all good things!). We would always hang out in the UT Austin Student Government and Senate of College Councils lounge and discuss your Communications classes and what we were going to do after graduating. I hope you're accomplishing those goals!

I cherish you and I want you to know our memories together hold a special place in my heart. You're included in the collective experiences that make me who I am today, and I am forever grateful.

— Austin Robinson

Send   Cancel

Friday, November 20th, 22:03

Brittany Wright,

If you're reading this, it's because you 'liked' a Facebook post I made back in 2018. I know it's been awhile, but I'm happy to present your very own webpage and my favorite memory with you!

My favorite memory with you is every time I was around you, whether it was in an APO meeting or just around campus. You have such an infectious personality and a rare heart that cares for every single person you meet. You're one of the only people I know who truly makes the life of every person you know better. I really hope you're living a better life than everyone else!

I cherish you and I want you to know our memories together hold a special place in my heart. You're included in the collective experiences that make me who I am today, and I am forever grateful.

– Austin Robinson

 Send   Cancel

Friday, November 20th, 22:07

Kevin Cook,

If you're reading this, it's because you 'liked' a Facebook post I made back in 2018. I know it's been awhile, but I'm happy to present your very own webpage and my favorite memory with you!

My favorite memory with you is the day I met you at Extreme Youth Leadership in 2011. From the second I heard your voice, I knew I loved you. The fact that we would later become friends was incredibly unlikely, but it happened. Now you're the only person I've turned mobile location services on for, and you constantly ask me why I am where I am. Kinda metaphorical!

I cherish you and I want you to know our memories together hold a special place in my heart. You're included in the collective experiences that make me who I am today, and I am forever grateful.

– Austin Robinson

 Send Cancel

Friday, November 20th, 22:10

Caleb Henderson,

If you're reading this, it's because you 'liked' a Facebook post I made back in 2018. I know it's been awhile, but I'm happy to present your very own webpage and my favorite memory with you!

My favorite memory with you is how supportive you were while I was running for Student Government Vice President at UT Austin. Basically anything I did in university, you were incredibly supportive of. I know I had a lot of people cheering me on, but you were one of the most sincere supporters. I thank you for every second you spent helping me grow!

I cherish you and I want you to know our memories together hold a special place in my heart. You're included in the collective experiences that make me who I am today, and I am forever grateful.

— Austin Robinson

Send   Cancel

Friday, November 20th, 22:13

Cassie Miller,

If you're reading this, it's because you 'liked' a Facebook post I made back in 2018. I know it's been awhile, but I'm happy to present your very own webpage and my favorite memory with you!

My favorite memory with you is how bad-ass you were at your job when we worked together at the skating rink. I know you were never appreciated by management, but your candidness and no-bullshit attitude with the customers was honestly refreshing. Those people can be real asshats. I know you're doing better than the rest of us, and then some!

I cherish you and I want you to know our memories together hold a special place in my heart. You're included in the collective experiences that make me who I am today, and I am forever grateful.

— Austin Robinson

Send   Cancel

Friday, November 20th, 22:15

Chandler Lopez,

If you're reading this, it's because you 'liked' a Facebook post I made back in 2018. I know it's been awhile, but I'm happy to present your very own webpage and my favorite memory with you!

You ALREADY know what I'm going to say. My favorite memory with you is when we went to that Yung Lean concert in Austin, Texas. We had basically never hung out in person before (sans university sightings), so what an amazing introduction to our friendship. And now you're onto bigger and better things in New York City of all places. Jealous!

I cherish you and I want you to know our memories together hold a special place in my heart. You're included in the collective experiences that make me who I am today, and I am forever grateful.

— Austin Robinson

Send   Cancel

Chazz Morgan,

If you're reading this, it's because you 'liked' a Facebook post I made back in 2018. I know it's been awhile, but I'm happy to present your very own webpage and my favorite memory with you!

My favorite memory with you is when we would hang out as children at the skating rink and share candy and play Pokémon together. I can't believe I would then go on to officiate your current wife's wedding with another man (before y'all's marriage, of course). It's funny how things all come together and work out. I hope y'all are happy and there are many more memories to come!

I cherish you and I want you to know our memories together hold a special place in my heart. You're included in the collective experiences that make me who I am today, and I am forever grateful.

– Austin Robinson

Send   Cancel

Friday, November 20th, 22:21

Che Coleman,

If you're reading this, it's because you 'liked' a Facebook post I made back in 2018. I know it's been awhile, but I'm happy to present your very own webpage and my favorite memory with you!

We've only met once, but my favorite memory with you is when you stopped in Brownwood with our mutual friend just to say hi to me as y'all were driving back to Austin from a roadtrip across the West. I'm glad I got to meet and know you for those 10 minutes, even if we never meet again. However, if we do, let it be for longer than that!

I cherish you and I want you to know our memories together hold a special place in my heart. You're included in the collective experiences that make me who I am today, and I am forever grateful.

— Austin Robinson

Send   Cancel

Friday, November 20th, 22:26

Chelsea Wilson,

If you're reading this, it's because you 'liked' a Facebook post I made back in 2018. I know it's been awhile, but I'm happy to present your very own webpage and my favorite memory with you!

My favorite memory with you is our entire childhood and the fact that you were my ride-or-die from ages 12 to 22. I know we hardly talk anymore, but you completely inspired my last Friendship Project book, and you're a huge reason that I even write and publish my own book, albeit how silly they are. I know we may never talk again, but I hope you achieve everything you want!

I cherish you and I want you to know our memories together hold a special place in my heart. You're included in the collective experiences that make me who I am today, and I am forever grateful.

– Austin Robinson

 Send   Cancel

Friday, November 20th, 22:29

Chelsea Hill,

If you're reading this, it's because you 'liked' a Facebook post I made back in 2018. I know it's been awhile, but I'm happy to present your very own webpage and my favorite memory with you!

My favorite memory with you is when you were my Senior Facilitator at the HOBY Texas North seminar and you kind of just let me do whatever he hell I wanted. I'm not entirely sure how you got involved with HOBY, but you are one of the rare volunteers that that organization needs to balance out the intense people it consistently attracts. It was so refreshing to meet you!

I cherish you and I want you to know our memories together hold a special place in my heart. You're included in the collective experiences that make me who I am today, and I am forever grateful.

– Austin Robinson

Send   Cancel

Friday, November 20th, 22:31

Cheyenne Bell,

If you're reading this, it's because you 'liked' a Facebook post I made back in 2018. I know it's been awhile, but I'm happy to present your very own webpage and my favorite memory with you!

My favorite memory with you is all the times we spent together in middle and high school and how incredibly happy you always were. You laugh a lot, and that's a great quality in a person. You aren't afraid to take the leap and move to somewhere new, do something different, or figure things out. I admire that in a person because it was hard for me to find the same attributes in myself!

I cherish you and I want you to know our memories together hold a special place in my heart. You're included in the collective experiences that make me who I am today, and I am forever grateful.

— Austin Robinson

 Send   Cancel

Friday, November 20th, 22:33

Chris Jenkins,

If you're reading this, it's because you 'liked' a Facebook post I made back in 2018. I know it's been awhile, but I'm happy to present your very own webpage and my favorite memory with you!

Oh my gosh, truly the only memory I have with you is when I printed off a tiny picture of myself and then glued it to a tiny sims-like structure, essentially making a mini version of myself. And then you wore it as a necklace around your neck during lunch. So I guess thank you for being the only person in my life to ever wear me as a necklace. It means a lot!

I cherish you and I want you to know our memories together hold a special place in my heart. You're included in the collective experiences that make me who I am today, and I am forever grateful.

– Austin Robinson

Send   Cancel

Friday, November 20th, 22:36

Chris Moore,

If you're reading this, it's because you 'liked' a Facebook post I made back in 2018. I know it's been awhile, but I'm happy to present your very own webpage and my favorite memory with you!

My favorite memory with you is when we almost dated and you forced me to watch that one Amazon Prime Video comedy show (everyone knows what I'm talking about, probably) on our first date. And now you're an incredible photographer and have the most aesthetically-pleasing photographs on your social medias. I just know you're going to make someone happy someday!

I cherish you and I want you to know our memories together hold a special place in my heart. You're included in the collective experiences that make me who I am today, and I am forever grateful.

— Austin Robinson

Send   Cancel

Friday, November 20th, 22:38

Chris Whitier,

If you're reading this, it's because you 'liked' a Facebook post I made back in 2018. I know it's been awhile, but I'm happy to present your very own webpage and my favorite memory with you!

You were the most interesting person I ever met while in high school, even though we didn't even go to the same high school. Everyone knew you as the person who could make them laugh, smile, and question your sanity. And that's what I call a triple threat! You're one of the few people who I think about and say, "I really wish I could know them today as I knew them back then!"

I cherish you and I want you to know our memories together hold a special place in my heart. You're included in the collective experiences that make me who I am today, and I am forever grateful.

— Austin Robinson

Send   Cancel

Friday, November 20th, 22:40

Chris Anderson,

If you're reading this, it's because you 'liked' a Facebook post I made back in 2018. I know it's been awhile, but I'm happy to present your very own webpage and my favorite memory with you!

My favorite memory with you is when you taught me about financial responsibility and how to apply for my first ever credit card. That is one of the first moments when I truly felt like I was becoming more of an adult and learning how to be my own person. I know that seems so small, but learning to become more independent means the world to me, and you facilitated that!

I cherish you and I want you to know our memories together hold a special place in my heart. You're included in the collective experiences that make me who I am today, and I am forever grateful.

— Austin Robinson

Friday, November 20th, 22:41

Chris Yardes,

If you're reading this, it's because you 'liked' a Facebook post I made back in 2018. I know it's been awhile, but I'm happy to present your very own webpage and my favorite memory with you!

My favorite memory with you is when I would see you in the McComb's School of Business and we would chat about your business degree. Because I was a social services major, business fascinated me so much. It was as if you took me into another reality and showed me what it was like in your world. I hope things are going well for you in your world!

I cherish you and I want you to know our memories together hold a special place in my heart. You're included in the collective experiences that make me who I am today, and I am forever grateful.

– Austin Robinson

Send   Cancel

Friday, November 20th, 22:44

Christina Scott,

If you're reading this, it's because you 'liked' a Facebook post I made back in 2018. I know it's been awhile, but I'm happy to present your very own webpage and my favorite memory with you!

You were one of the best friends I've ever had in my life. I know we don't talk much anymore, but we still check in every once in awhile. You're getting married soon and I truly can't wait to support you in any way you'd like. My favorite memory is when we stayed up all night designing and creating my APO Banquet outfit, which was so ridiculous!

I cherish you and I want you to know our memories together hold a special place in my heart. You're included in the collective experiences that make me who I am today, and I am forever grateful.

— Austin Robinson

Friday, November 20th, 22:46

Colin Murphy,

If you're reading this, it's because you 'liked' a Facebook post I made back in 2018. I know it's been awhile, but I'm happy to present your very own webpage and my favorite memory with you!

My favorite memory with you is when we spent time together at the HOBY Maryland conference back in 2015 (I think that's the right year??? Who can never be sure). You were an incredible roommate and I can't believe we're still connected to this day! Also, you're still the only person I've ever met that has a last name that is my first name. Absolutely iconic!

I cherish you and I want you to know our memories together hold a special place in my heart. You're included in the collective experiences that make me who I am today, and I am forever grateful.

– Austin Robinson

Send   Cancel

Friday, November 20th, 22:48

Crystin Perries,

If you're reading this, it's because you 'liked' a Facebook post I made back in 2018. I know it's been awhile, but I'm happy to present your very own webpage and my favorite memory with you!

You are the best person I've ever met in my entire life. And that is NOT an exaggeration, and you won't see me saying that about anyone else in this book (sorry everyone else). My favorite memory with you is when you asked me for my phone number in 6th grade and I tried to give you one of those fake numbers that tells you you've been rejected. Sorry!

I cherish you and I want you to know our memories together hold a special place in my heart. You're included in the collective experiences that make me who I am today, and I am forever grateful.

— Austin Robinson

Dang Taylor,

If you're reading this, it's because you 'liked' a Facebook post I made back in 2018. I know it's been awhile, but I'm happy to present your very own webpage and my favorite memory with you!

My favorite memory with you is when you would bring a stuffed llama around to every event while in university. You knew how to immediately brighten up people's days, whether it was through that llama or through your accepting and welcoming personality. I hope someday you own a real llama, although I wouldn't be surprised if you already do!

I cherish you and I want you to know our memories together hold a special place in my heart. You're included in the collective experiences that make me who I am today, and I am forever grateful.

— Austin Robinson

Send   Cancel

Saturday, November 21st, 09:40

Daniel Green,

If you're reading this, it's because you 'liked' a Facebook post I made back in 2018. I know it's been awhile, but I'm happy to present your very own webpage and my favorite memory with you!

My favorite memory with you is when we ran for UT Austin Student Body President and Vice President together, AND GOT LAST PLACE. It's probably because our only campaign strategies were to set up a tent outside of the university gym to live in for two weeks, and to give away slap bracelets to every student. Oh well, I guess you live and you learn!

I cherish you and I want you to know our memories together hold a special place in my heart. You're included in the collective experiences that make me who I am today, and I am forever grateful.

– Austin Robinson

Saturday, November 21st, 09:43

Daniel Bailey,

If you're reading this, it's because you 'liked' a Facebook post I made back in 2018. I know it's been awhile, but I'm happy to present your very own webpage and my favorite memory with you!

I have absolutely no clue who you are, but it looks like we've been friends on Facebook since February 2016. I don't recognize where you're from or the university you went to. We don't even have messages together. This is truly a mystery, and I'm not sure why you 'liked' my Facebook post, but thanks! I guess if you want to become BEST FRIENDS, LET ME KNOW!

I cherish you and I want you to know our memories together hold a special place in my heart. You're included in the collective experiences that make me who I am today, and I am forever grateful.

– Austin Robinson

Saturday, November 21st, 09:48

Daniel Powell,

If you're reading this, it's because you 'liked' a Facebook post I made back in 2018. I know it's been awhile, but I'm happy to present your very own webpage and my favorite memory with you!

Okay so you're my ex and we don't even talk anymore, but hiii. My favorite memory with you is probably when we used to play Town of Salem together. I haven't played since we broke up, but I truly think about playing it so often because it was so fun. I guess that new game 'Among Us' is similar, but it does not look fun at all to me. Too much jumping around and going into vents!

I cherish you and I want you to know our memories together hold a special place in my heart. You're included in the collective experiences that make me who I am today, and I am forever grateful.

— Austin Robinson

Saturday, November 21st, 09:50

Daniel Andrews,

If you're reading this, it's because you 'liked' a Facebook post I made back in 2018. I know it's been awhile, but I'm happy to present your very own webpage and my favorite memory with you!

Oh my gosh, I have not talked to you in so long! Wow, we truly had a wild ride together: from almost dating to you dating my best friend to all the other things that I can't mention here. My favorite memory with you is when we had that party at our mutual friend's dad's apartment in our hometown (well I guess your hometown is LA, but yeah). I hope you're doing well!

I cherish you and I want you to know our memories together hold a special place in my heart. You're included in the collective experiences that make me who I am today, and I am forever grateful.

– Austin Robinson

Saturday, November 21st, 10:15

Danny Adams,

If you're reading this, it's because you 'liked' a Facebook post I made back in 2018. I know it's been awhile, but I'm happy to present your very own webpage and my favorite memory with you!

My favorite memory with you is all those nights you would host Super Smash Bros tournaments at your apartment! You were always one of the nicest people at the university, and it's amazing how many people liked you and wanted to be around you. I hope you have people in your life today that appreciate you the way we all did back then!

I cherish you and I want you to know our memories together hold a special place in my heart. You're included in the collective experiences that make me who I am today, and I am forever grateful.

– Austin Robinson

Saturday, November 21st, 10:18

Dave Rivera,

If you're reading this, it's because you 'liked' a Facebook post I made back in 2018. I know it's been awhile, but I'm happy to present your very own webpage and my favorite memory with you!

My favorite memory with you is when we met in Hollywood and then a year later I almost became your roommate! I still receive notifications for the songs that you put up on SoundCloud. I think it's amazing that you're following your passion in an unconventional field in none other than Los Angeles. A lot of people can't say the same, so I hope you're living it up!

I cherish you and I want you to know our memories together hold a special place in my heart. You're included in the collective experiences that make me who I am today, and I am forever grateful.

— Austin Robinson

Saturday, November 21st, 10:21

David Long,

If you're reading this, it's because you 'liked' a Facebook post I made back in 2018. I know it's been awhile, but I'm happy to present your very own webpage and my favorite memory with you!

My favorite memory with you is when I was drunk for one of the first times in my life ever (like, black out drunk), and we met on the street. I truly can't remember much at all, but I found it so funny and we bounded after that. Sometimes the greatest memories are the ones you can't remember and when you're drunk, LOL. At least we'll always have that!

I cherish you and I want you to know our memories together hold a special place in my heart. You're included in the collective experiences that make me who I am today, and I am forever grateful.

– Austin Robinson

Saturday, November 21st, 10:22

David Thomas,

If you're reading this, it's because you 'liked' a Facebook post I made back in 2018. I know it's been awhile, but I'm happy to present your very own webpage and my favorite memory with you!

My favorite memory with you is when we were sitting alone in the Liberal Arts building at UT Austin and you told me that you thought I was a marketing genius with my AUSTIN JAMES ROBINSON brand. It was truly the first time anyone had expressed that they were in awe by all of the projects I do and the stamina I have. And I had truly never thought about it before. Thanks!

I cherish you and I want you to know our memories together hold a special place in my heart. You're included in the collective experiences that make me who I am today, and I am forever grateful.

— Austin Robinson

Saturday, November 21st, 10:24

David Baker,

If you're reading this, it's because you 'liked' a Facebook post I made back in 2018. I know it's been awhile, but I'm happy to present your very own webpage and my favorite memory with you!

My favorite memory with you is when we met in Cross County class at UT Austin and then realized we were from the same rural area of Texas. It was wild because virtually no one at UT is from our neck of the woods. Then I knew I had at least one friend in Cross Country, a class I knew no one in and had no business taking, LOL. But at least it brought me to you!

I cherish you and I want you to know our memories together hold a special place in my heart. You're included in the collective experiences that make me who I am today, and I am forever grateful.

— Austin Robinson

Saturday, November 21st, 10:27

Dawn Cooper,

If you're reading this, it's because you 'liked' a Facebook post I made back in 2018. I know it's been awhile, but I'm happy to present your very own webpage and my favorite memory with you!

My favorite memory with you is when we talked about our prospective career paths and how similar they were. You're now such a successful Music Therapist for children with disabilities! And I'm working as a Developmental Disabilities Service Coordinator. I'm glad I have friends who have the same passion for helping underprivileged populations!

I cherish you and I want you to know our memories together hold a special place in my heart. You're included in the collective experiences that make me who I am today, and I am forever grateful.

— Austin Robinson

Saturday, November 21st, 10:29

Destiny Patterson,

If you're reading this, it's because you 'liked' a Facebook post I made back in 2018. I know it's been awhile, but I'm happy to present your very own webpage and my favorite memory with you!

My favorite memory with you is when we grew up together and collectively experienced so much. You showed me the 'Left Behind' books when we were just in primary school, and I still find them so fascinating, albeit not believing in the overall theme. Likewise, we would always go to the skating rink as kids, so there's a special bond there that can never be broken!

I cherish you and I want you to know our memories together hold a special place in my heart. You're included in the collective experiences that make me who I am today, and I am forever grateful.

— Austin Robinson

Saturday, November 21st, 10:31

Divine Jackson,

If you're reading this, it's because you 'liked' a Facebook post I made back in 2018. I know it's been awhile, but I'm happy to present your very own webpage and my favorite memory with you!

My favorite memory with you is when you continually supported me throughout my UT Austin Student Government career, even though I never held a position and you never endorsed me, LOL. I never minded that because I was always running as a joke, but you still always believed that I could do great things no matter what the outcome. You're great!

I cherish you and I want you to know our memories together hold a special place in my heart. You're included in the collective experiences that make me who I am today, and I am forever grateful.

— Austin Robinson

Saturday, November 21st, 10:34

Drew Gonzalez,

If you're reading this, it's because you 'liked' a Facebook post I made back in 2018. I know it's been awhile, but I'm happy to present your very own webpage and my favorite memory with you!

My favorite memory with you is when you were one of the fellow emo boys in middle school, so I felt like I had a kinship with you solely based on that. You were always best friends with all of my best friends. And while we weren't best friends, we had hella respect for each other. To this day, you're still super cool and forging your own path for yourself!

I cherish you and I want you to know our memories together hold a special place in my heart. You're included in the collective experiences that make me who I am today, and I am forever grateful.

— Austin Robinson

Saturday, November 21st, 10:38

Eddie Richardson,

If you're reading this, it's because you 'liked' a Facebook post I made back in 2018. I know it's been awhile, but I'm happy to present your very own webpage and my favorite memory with you!

My favorite memory with you is when we went to The Cheesecake Factory in Pasadena, California because I was obsessed with taking every single Texas Blazer there and we didn't get the chance to go while in university! I know we've been planning a second trip to The Cheesecake Factory since the first one three years ago, but I just know it's going to happen!

I cherish you and I want you to know our memories together hold a special place in my heart. You're included in the collective experiences that make me who I am today, and I am forever grateful.

— Austin Robinson

Saturday, November 21st, 10:40

Ella Hughes,

If you're reading this, it's because you 'liked' a Facebook post I made back in 2018. I know it's been awhile, but I'm happy to present your very own webpage and my favorite memory with you!

OMG, you're literally a drag queen! I think your real persona is also in these webpages, so I guess you're getting two! My favorite memory with you is when we matched on JSwipe two separate times and had SO much in common. And the fact that we had mutual friends in San Antonio. I'm sorry I couldn't come see you in Cincinnati when I was staying in Chicago!

I cherish you and I want you to know our memories together hold a special place in my heart. You're included in the collective experiences that make me who I am today, and I am forever grateful.

— Austin Robinson

Saturday, November 21st, 10:42

Elvis White,

If you're reading this, it's because you 'liked' a Facebook post I made back in 2018. I know it's been awhile, but I'm happy to present your very own webpage and my favorite memory with you!

My favorite memory with you is when we were classmates together in the UT Austin McComb's School of Business Foundations of Business Summer School Program. I ended up dropping out, but I believe you graduated because you're a bad-ass and smart. You always played Devil's Advocate with people's point of views, and it was refreshing to have a different opinion on things!

I cherish you and I want you to know our memories together hold a special place in my heart. You're included in the collective experiences that make me who I am today, and I am forever grateful.

— Austin Robinson

Saturday, November 21st, 10:45

Emmanuelle Nelson,

If you're reading this, it's because you 'liked' a Facebook post I made back in 2018. I know it's been awhile, but I'm happy to present your very own webpage and my favorite memory with you!

We've never met, but you're such good friends with our mutual friend Avery! And I respect that because Avery is such a unique and incredible person. I always appreciate your social media posts about social issues and your continued awareness on gender expression. Also you're very funny, so I kind of hate that we've never met each other in person before!

I cherish you and I want you to know our memories together hold a special place in my heart. You're included in the collective experiences that make me who I am today, and I am forever grateful.

— Austin Robinson

Saturday, November 21st, 10:50

Garrett Cox,

If you're reading this, it's because you 'liked' a Facebook post I made back in 2018. I know it's been awhile, but I'm happy to present your very own webpage and my favorite memory with you!

My favorite memory with you is how incredibly kind, nice, and supportive you were with every single person you met in Texas Blazers and at the University. I'm not sure I've ever met a happier human being than you, and I'm sure I won't ever again. You're a special breed, and I hope you remain that way forever. Keep doing what you're doing!

I cherish you and I want you to know our memories together hold a special place in my heart. You're included in the collective experiences that make me who I am today, and I am forever grateful.

— Austin Robinson

Saturday, November 21st, 10:52

Garrett Flores,

If you're reading this, it's because you 'liked' a Facebook post I made back in 2018. I know it's been awhile, but I'm happy to present your very own webpage and my favorite memory with you!

My favorite memory with you is when we were in Key Club together, but in different states! I absolutely adored meeting Key Club members from different districts, states, and nations. I felt so close to them and I would sometimes become pen pals with them. And you were one of the first ever people to own an AUSTIN JAMES ROBINSON t-shirt. So congrats for that!

I cherish you and I want you to know our memories together hold a special place in my heart. You're included in the collective experiences that make me who I am today, and I am forever grateful.

— Austin Robinson

Saturday, November 21st, 10:54

Grant Harris,

If you're reading this, it's because you 'liked' a Facebook post I made back in 2018. I know it's been awhile, but I'm happy to present your very own webpage and my favorite memory with you!

I don't know who you are and we've never spoken before, but from the looks of our mutual friends on Facebook, you were in Student Government so we probably added each other because of common interests. It seems like you're still passionate about politics and changing the world, so I'm glad to see that. Maybe our paths will finally cross one day!

I cherish you and I want you to know our memories together hold a special place in my heart. You're included in the collective experiences that make me who I am today, and I am forever grateful.

— Austin Robinson

Send   Cancel

Saturday, November 21st, 10:57

Gregory Carter,

If you're reading this, it's because you 'liked' a Facebook post I made back in 2018. I know it's been awhile, but I'm happy to present your very own webpage and my favorite memory with you!

I love you so much. I have so many amazing memories with you that I can't possibly pick just one to stand out. So I would say my favorite memory is when you called me to ask if you should take a corporate position or a nonprofit position in your field. It was such an important conversation, and you knew I would be the perfect person to have it with. I can't wait to see you again!

I cherish you and I want you to know our memories together hold a special place in my heart. You're included in the collective experiences that make me who I am today, and I am forever grateful.

— Austin Robinson

Saturday, November 21st, 11:18

Hannah Howard,

If you're reading this, it's because you 'liked' a Facebook post I made back in 2018. I know it's been awhile, but I'm happy to present your very own webpage and my favorite memory with you!

I can't believe we've known each other since SIXTH GRADE. That is, like, 100 years basically. My favorite memory with you is when I used to look up that website of your name as the URL and it was owned by a 10 year old girl in the UK. My middle school brain thought that was the funniest thing in existence for whatever reason. Also, all of the late night phone conversations we had!

I cherish you and I want you to know our memories together hold a special place in my heart. You're included in the collective experiences that make me who I am today, and I am forever grateful.

– Austin Robinson

Saturday, November 21st, 11:21

Hannah Washington,

If you're reading this, it's because you 'liked' a Facebook post I made back in 2018. I know it's been awhile, but I'm happy to present your very own webpage and my favorite memory with you!

OMG, you're the original Horse Girl to me, because I truly had never met one before and you're the first for me. My favorite memory with you is when we attended the first ever - and basically one of the last - HOBY Advanced Leadership Academies together. I can't believe we were part of one of the most unique parts of HOBY's history - and our own!

I cherish you and I want you to know our memories together hold a special place in my heart. You're included in the collective experiences that make me who I am today, and I am forever grateful.

— Austin Robinson

Saturday, November 21st, 11:25

Hannah Martin,

If you're reading this, it's because you 'liked' a Facebook post I made back in 2018. I know it's been awhile, but I'm happy to present your very own webpage and my favorite memory with you!

My favorite memory with you is how involved you were in APO - you basically OWNED that organization, for real. You were the person I respected the most because you were the only one willing to progress it and push it forward, while the rest of us were simply having fun. Thank you for holding the structure together for the rest of us - it was important!

I cherish you and I want you to know our memories together hold a special place in my heart. You're included in the collective experiences that make me who I am today, and I am forever grateful.

– Austin Robinson

Send   Cancel

Saturday, November 21st, 11:26

Hannah Mitchell,

If you're reading this, it's because you 'liked' a Facebook post I made back in 2018. I know it's been awhile, but I'm happy to present your very own webpage and my favorite memory with you!

My favorite memory with you is when I spontaneous moved to Portland, Oregon and you randomly had a place for me to stay a 4-minute walk away from my work-place. It was a total punk house filled with weirdos and I basically slept on the floor for four months. That period in my life feels like a fever dream, I'm sure for the both of us. Let's do it again someday!

I cherish you and I want you to know our memories together hold a special place in my heart. You're included in the collective experiences that make me who I am today, and I am forever grateful.

— Austin Robinson

Saturday, November 21st, 11:28

Hannah Ward,

If you're reading this, it's because you 'liked' a Facebook post I made back in 2018. I know it's been awhile, but I'm happy to present your very own webpage and my favorite memory with you!

My favorite memory with you is when we attended the HOBY Texas North seminar together as leadership volunteers. I mean, at first you were my superior because I was an ambassador going through the program. But then we spent many years together volunteering to make the seminar great for the ambassadors that came after us. I miss that and hope we can do it again soon!

I cherish you and I want you to know our memories together hold a special place in my heart. You're included in the collective experiences that make me who I am today, and I am forever grateful.

- Austin Robinson

Saturday, November 21st, 11:30

Hardeep Butler,

If you're reading this, it's because you 'liked' a Facebook post I made back in 2018. I know it's been awhile, but I'm happy to present your very own webpage and my favorite memory with you!

My favorite memory with you is when we matched on Tinder while I was doing Study Abroad in Oxford, England! I'm so glad we got to hang out so much in London and that you're basically the only person I texted on my UK pay-as-you-go flip phone. You're also the only person I know who speaks FIVE language and is also cool. Hope you're keeping the UK cool!

I cherish you and I want you to know our memories together hold a special place in my heart. You're included in the collective experiences that make me who I am today, and I am forever grateful.

– Austin Robinson

Saturday, November 21st, 11:34

Harvey Thompson,

If you're reading this, it's because you 'liked' a Facebook post I made back in 2018. I know it's been awhile, but I'm happy to present your very own webpage and my favorite memory with you!

I know we're friends on Facebook and have a ton of UT connections, but I don't think we ever met or know each other that well. You probably 'liked' my Facebook post because you thought it was a joke. But joke's on you because now I'm writing you a webpage and rambling on in order to hit my word quota. Or maybe the joke's on me. Oops, gotta go - bye!

I cherish you and I want you to know our memories together hold a special place in my heart. You're included in the collective experiences that make me who I am today, and I am forever grateful.

— Austin Robinson

Send   Cancel

Saturday, November 21st, 11:37

Hasan Perez,

If you're reading this, it's because you 'liked' a Facebook post I made back in 2018. I know it's been awhile, but I'm happy to present your very own webpage and my favorite memory with you!

My favorite memory with you is when we would hang out in the UT Austin Student Government and Senate of College Councils lounge and discuss the politics of the student body and who is best equipped to handle the needs of the students. While you weren't involved in my campaign to become Student Body Vice President, you were always supportive of me!

I cherish you and I want you to know our memories together hold a special place in my heart. You're included in the collective experiences that make me who I am today, and I am forever grateful.

— Austin Robinson

Saturday, November 21st, 11:38

Haylie Torres,

If you're reading this, it's because you 'liked' a Facebook post I made back in 2018. I know it's been awhile, but I'm happy to present your very own webpage and my favorite memory with you!

Wow, it has been SO long since I have talked to you! We went to high school together, which feels like forever ago. My favorite memory with you is how sweet and smiley you were in high school. I know we didn't have a lot of mutual friends, but everyone respected and liked you because of how welcoming you were. It's rare to find someone like that, especially in high school!

I cherish you and I want you to know our memories together hold a special place in my heart. You're included in the collective experiences that make me who I am today, and I am forever grateful.

— Austin Robinson

 Send   Cancel

Saturday, November 21st, 11:41

Humza Simmons,

If you're reading this, it's because you 'liked' a Facebook post I made back in 2018. I know it's been awhile, but I'm happy to present your very own webpage and my favorite memory with you!

I don't know who you are and we're no longer friends on Facebook! Sad! I guess I can't really say anything about our friendship, but regardless I hope you're doing amazing in life and that you're going after everything you ever wanted. Or maybe you're content in being where you are, and in that case I hope you remain the same. Just do whatever you want!

I cherish you and I want you to know our memories together hold a special place in my heart. You're included in the collective experiences that make me who I am today, and I am forever grateful.

– Austin Robinson

Saturday, November 21st, 11:44

Ian Garcia,

If you're reading this, it's because you 'liked' a Facebook post I made back in 2018. I know it's been awhile, but I'm happy to present your very own webpage and my favorite memory with you!

We never got to hang out, but I remember matching with you on Tinder and you being a medical student at UT Austin! From Facebook, it looks like you ended up getting your medical degree and now you're in residency. I really hope that's going well and that you become a kick-ass doctor someday that saves so much lives. I look forward to seeing it!

I cherish you and I want you to know our memories together hold a special place in my heart. You're included in the collective experiences that make me who I am today, and I am forever grateful.

— Austin Robinson

Saturday, November 21st, 11:46

Ian Roberts,

If you're reading this, it's because you 'liked' a Facebook post I made back in 2018. I know it's been awhile, but I'm happy to present your very own webpage and my favorite memory with you!

My favorite memory with you is meeting you at the HOBY Texas Gulf Coast seminar down in Galveston. I accidentally drove to Corpus Christi because the only instructions I had were "The A&M campus on an island" LOL. Anyway, you were my favorite ambassador because of how vivacious you are. We had such a great connection and I'm glad we're still connected.

I cherish you and I want you to know our memories together hold a special place in my heart. You're included in the collective experiences that make me who I am today, and I am forever grateful.

— Austin Robinson

 Send Cancel

Saturday, November 21st, 11:50

Jacob Peterson,

If you're reading this, it's because you 'liked' a Facebook post I made back in 2018. I know it's been awhile, but I'm happy to present your very own webpage and my favorite memory with you!

I thoroughly enjoy hanging out with Max, you, and the crew every single time I come to Tucson, Arizona. My favorite memory with you is when we ate at the Waffle House and ordered, like, an absurd amount of food. And we thought their advertisement of "16 MEALS FOR $6!" was so funny because it sounded like we would get that much food for $6 total!

I cherish you and I want you to know our memories together hold a special place in my heart. You're included in the collective experiences that make me who I am today, and I am forever grateful.

– Austin Robinson

Send   Cancel

Saturday, November 21st, 11:52

Jasleen Foster,

If you're reading this, it's because you 'liked' a Facebook post I made back in 2018. I know it's been awhile, but I'm happy to present your very own webpage and my favorite memory with you!

My favorite memory with you is when we would hang out in the UT Austin Student Government and Senate of College Councils lounge together with the rest of the student body crew and just talk about all of our passions and goals while at the university. I know you achieved all of yours - that's just who you are. I definitely can't say the same, so I respect you!

I cherish you and I want you to know our memories together hold a special place in my heart. You're included in the collective experiences that make me who I am today, and I am forever grateful.

— Austin Robinson

Saturday, November 21st, 11:55

Jason Martinez,

If you're reading this, it's because you 'liked' a Facebook post I made back in 2018. I know it's been awhile, but I'm happy to present your very own webpage and my favorite memory with you!

My favorite memory with you is how excited you were for my former Friendship Project 'Project Letters' to the point where you wanted a say in what was put in it and where your letter was located in the book. I loved the initiative and how excited you were for my various passion projects I conducted at UT Austin. I'm sorry I never made you your own t-shirt!

I cherish you and I want you to know our memories together hold a special place in my heart. You're included in the collective experiences that make me who I am today, and I am forever grateful.

– Austin Robinson

Send   Cancel

Saturday, November 21st, 11:56

Jay Turner,

If you're reading this, it's because you 'liked' a Facebook post I made back in 2018. I know it's been awhile, but I'm happy to present your very own webpage and my favorite memory with you!

My favorite memory with you is how you came to me to ask the best way to get into Texas Blazers and position yourself for success within UT Austin. I never had many people come to me to ask for school advice because they mainly thought I joked all the time - so that was refreshing! You also supported my AUSTIN JAMES ROBINSON brand so much!

I cherish you and I want you to know our memories together hold a special place in my heart. You're included in the collective experiences that make me who I am today, and I am forever grateful.

— Austin Robinson

 Send Cancel

Saturday, November 21st, 11:58

Joanne Gray,

If you're reading this, it's because you 'liked' a Facebook post I made back in 2018. I know it's been awhile, but I'm happy to present your very own webpage and my favorite memory with you!

You are literally so good at everything you do. My favorite memory with you is just seeing all of your amazing artistic and funny posts on various social media sites. You make art, you make music, you make memes. Truly a triple threat. And you're invested in social issues and spreading awareness about different gender expressions. Your presence on this earth is definitely needed!

I cherish you and I want you to know our memories together hold a special place in my heart. You're included in the collective experiences that make me who I am today, and I am forever grateful.

– Austin Robinson

 Send   Cancel

Saturday, November 21st, 18:07

Joel Gonzalez,

If you're reading this, it's because you 'liked' a Facebook post I made back in 2018. I know it's been awhile, but I'm happy to present your very own webpage and my favorite memory with you!

I don't really know you too well, but we went to school together and you were one of the cool STEM people. My favorite memory with you is when you asked me if I would design and write you a résumé! You kncw I was getting into résumé designing and it was such good practice. I hope you ended up using it and that it got you the job you wanted!

I cherish you and I want you to know our memories together hold a special place in my heart. You're included in the collective experiences that make me who I am today, and I am forever grateful.

— Austin Robinson

Send   Cancel

Saturday, November 21st, 18:09

Jonny Robinson,

If you're reading this, it's because you 'liked' a Facebook post I made back in 2018. I know it's been awhile, but I'm happy to present your very own webpage and my favorite memory with you!

OMG I can't believe I already wrote one of these for your drag queen persona and now here I am making one for YOU. Gosh, I guess you're kind of the same person as your drag queen persona, so I kind of already gave my favorite memory with you. So I'm going to keep writing until my word quota is reached and oh look there time is up - bye bye!

I cherish you and I want you to know our memories together hold a special place in my heart. You're included in the collective experiences that make me who I am today, and I am forever grateful.

– Austin Robinson

Send   Cancel

Saturday, November 21st, 18:10

Jordan Phillips,

If you're reading this, it's because you 'liked' a Facebook post I made back in 2018. I know it's been awhile, but I'm happy to present your very own webpage and my favorite memory with you!

My favorite memory with you is when we accidentally got trapped in the middle of no-where Kansas on a military base for 2 weeks straight. Anyone else reading is gonna want a memoir detailing the event, and honestly we should give it to them! I gained major respect for every single person who we were with for those two weeks. It was so unexpected, but one of my fondest memories!

I cherish you and I want you to know our memories together hold a special place in my heart. You're included in the collective experiences that make me who I am today, and I am forever grateful.

– Austin Robinson

Send   Cancel

Saturday, November 21st, 18:12

Jordee Ramirez,

If you're reading this, it's because you 'liked' a Facebook post I made back in 2018. I know it's been awhile, but I'm happy to present your very own webpage and my favorite memory with you!

My favorite memory with you is when we were on the President Student Advisory Committee at UT Austin, and we got to meet with President Fenves every couple of months to advocate for the students of UT. It was incredibly wild that I was even on that committee - and it was all thanks to my ironic run for Student Body Vice President. I had fun with you!

I cherish you and I want you to know our memories together hold a special place in my heart. You're included in the collective experiences that make me who I am today, and I am forever grateful.

– Austin Robinson

Send   Cancel

Joshua Bryant,

If you're reading this, it's because you 'liked' a Facebook post I made back in 2018. I know it's been awhile, but I'm happy to present your very own webpage and my favorite memory with you!

Wow, I have truly known you for SO long, and we have way too many memories together. Like, we were basically attached at the hip for the last couple of years of high school. If I had to choose, my favorite memory with you is when you filmed me making YouTube videos in your family's hot tub because absolutely why NOT. You're one of my favorite people forever!

I cherish you and I want you to know our memories together hold a special place in my heart. You're included in the collective experiences that make me who I am today, and I am forever grateful.

– Austin Robinson

Send   Cancel

Saturday, November 21st, 18:16

Julio Clark,

If you're reading this, it's because you 'liked' a Facebook post I made back in 2018. I know it's been awhile, but I'm happy to present your very own webpage and my favorite memory with you!

Okay, I truly do not know who you are, but it looks like we connected on Facebook because of Alpha Phi Omega at one point! Which was such a fun time in our university careers, so let's talk about that! I can't believe the UT Austin APO chapter had 500 members... like, that's almost as many people as I went to high school with. Such a huge and diverse organization!

I cherish you and I want you to know our memories together hold a special place in my heart. You're included in the collective experiences that make me who I am today, and I am forever grateful.

— Austin Robinson

Send   Cancel

Saturday, November 21st, 18:22

Justin Campbell,

If you're reading this, it's because you 'liked' a Facebook post I made back in 2018. I know it's been awhile, but I'm happy to present your very own webpage and my favorite memory with you!

My favorite memory with you HAS GOT to be when I officiated your wedding with your NOW EX WIFE. The best part is that both of you allowed me to wear my AUSTIN JAMES ROBINSON shirt and make it an official AJR themed wedding. I was so sad that y'all got divorced only a year later. I hope my themed wedding didn't curse y'all!

I cherish you and I want you to know our memories together hold a special place in my heart. You're included in the collective experiences that make me who I am today, and I am forever grateful.

— Austin Robinson

 Send Cancel

Saturday, November 21st, 18:24

Justin James,

If you're reading this, it's because you 'liked' a Facebook post I made back in 2018. I know it's been awhile, but I'm happy to present your very own webpage and my favorite memory with you!

This is gonna be a little bit TMI, but my favorite memory with you is when you were house-sitting for our mutual friend, but asked me to come over and hook up in their house. Looking back, maybe we shouldn't have because what if they had a house camera. But I don't think you ever got in trouble, so I guess it worked out. Thanks for that thrill, I guess!

I cherish you and I want you to know our memories together hold a special place in my heart. You're included in the collective experiences that make me who I am today, and I am forever grateful.

– Austin Robinson

Send Cancel

Saturday, November 21st, 18:26

Kathryn Alexander,

If you're reading this, it's because you 'liked' a Facebook post I made back in 2018. I know it's been awhile, but I'm happy to present your very own webpage and my favorite memory with you!

You are TRULY one of the happiest people I have ever, ever, ever met. It's wild. Some might say uncanny. But I say totally canny! You brought smiles to the face of every person you interacted with in Alpha Phi Omega. You had huge dreams and I just know you're still chasing them, if you haven't already achieved them. I have no doubt about your outcome!

I cherish you and I want you to know our memories together hold a special place in my heart. You're included in the collective experiences that make me who I am today, and I am forever grateful.

– Austin Robinson

Send   Cancel

Saturday, November 21st, 18:28

Kathy Rodriguez,

If you're reading this, it's because you 'liked' a Facebook post I made back in 2018. I know it's been awhile, but I'm happy to present your very own webpage and my favorite memory with you!

ANOTHER CANADIAN. My absolute favorite - and probably sole - memory with you is when we attended the Circle K International Convention in 2015 (which tripled as the Key Club International Convention and the Kiwanis International Convention). I can't believe we had a "Western Themed" talent show and I won by representing your region, WESTERN CANADA lmaooo!

I cherish you and I want you to know our memories together hold a special place in my heart. You're included in the collective experiences that make me who I am today, and I am forever grateful.

– Austin Robinson

 Send   Cancel

Saturday, November 21st, 18:32

Katy Parker,

If you're reading this, it's because you 'liked' a Facebook post I made back in 2018. I know it's been awhile, but I'm happy to present your very own webpage and my favorite memory with you!

My favorite memory with you is when we decided to get parts of our bodies pierced in Oxford, England while we were doing Study Abroad. Probably in the middle of class time. I got a Smiley piercing and we totally freaked out the other students. Worth it. Thinking back on it, we probably should have calmed down significantly, but were we going to? NO!

I cherish you and I want you to know our memories together hold a special place in my heart. You're included in the collective experiences that make me who I am today, and I am forever grateful.

— Austin Robinson

Send   Cancel

Saturday, November 21st, 18:34

Kelley Watson,

If you're reading this, it's because you 'liked' a Facebook post I made back in 2018. I know it's been awhile, but I'm happy to present your very own webpage and my favorite memory with you!

My favorite memory with you is how sweet you were to every single person in Alpha Phi Omega. No matter who it was and how they treated you, you treated them with dignity and respect. You are a class act and I aspire to have the patience and sweetness that you have. I am learning to every day! I just know you are in the adult world making everyone around you happy!

I cherish you and I want you to know our memories together hold a special place in my heart. You're included in the collective experiences that make me who I am today, and I am forever grateful.

— Austin Robinson

Send   Cancel

99

Saturday, November 21st, 18:36

Kelly Russell,

If you're reading this, it's because you 'liked' a Facebook post I made back in 2018. I know it's been awhile, but I'm happy to present your very own webpage and my favorite memory with you!

My favorite memory with you is when we would hang out with the Texas Spirits as Texas Blazers and all have an amazing time. I believe me, you, and Ross hung out quite often, and it was always fun. Little moments like that from my university days is what made it one of the best experiences in my life. Thank you for making my memories and life a little better!

I cherish you and I want you to know our memories together hold a special place in my heart. You're included in the collective experiences that make me who I am today, and I am forever grateful.

— Austin Robinson

Send   Cancel

Saturday, November 21st, 18:38

Kennedy Lewis,

If you're reading this, it's because you 'liked' a Facebook post I made back in 2018. I know it's been awhile, but I'm happy to present your very own webpage and my favorite memory with you!

OMG I truly do not recognize your name at all and apparently I don't have a friend with your name on my Facebook account. So I have no clue what to do with this webpage. What about free publicity for my Publishing Press? Okay, everyone should go read my other books. I guess just go to Amazon and type in my name or ask me about them. Figure it out!

I cherish you and I want you to know our memories together hold a special place in my heart. You're included in the collective experiences that make me who I am today, and I am forever grateful.

— Austin Robinson

Send   Cancel

Saturday, November 21st, 18:41

Kevin Evans,

If you're reading this, it's because you 'liked' a Facebook post I made back in 2018. I know it's been awhile, but I'm happy to present your very own webpage and my favorite memory with you!

I love and miss you so much. I grew incredibly close to you during one of the hardest periods of my life. And even though we stopped hanging out shortly after, you will never know what that did for me. My favorite memory with you is going to a sports car viewing out in the middle of nowhere Texas and understanding car culture that you know so well!

I cherish you and I want you to know our memories together hold a special place in my heart. You're included in the collective experiences that make me who I am today, and I am forever grateful.

— Austin Robinson

Send   Cancel

Kizer Brooks,

If you're reading this, it's because you 'liked' a Facebook post I made back in 2018. I know it's been awhile, but I'm happy to present your very own webpage and my favorite memory with you!

My favorite memory with you is when I visited your apartment while I was "living" in Chicago for a hot minute. We had been internet friends for years, but had never met before. It was the perfect opportunity. You showed me all of your art projects and so many cool things in your place right off the Blue Line. It definitely made my extended Chicago trip worth it!

I cherish you and I want you to know our memories together hold a special place in my heart. You're included in the collective experiences that make me who I am today, and I am forever grateful.

— Austin Robinson

Send   Cancel

Saturday, November 21st, 18:44

Kort Griffin,

If you're reading this, it's because you 'liked' a Facebook post I made back in 2018. I know it's been awhile, but I'm happy to present your very own webpage and my favorite memory with you!

Although we've never met in person before, my favorite memory with you is when we would have long discussions about Alpha Phi Omega and what it was like back in your day compared to my present day. You always made me wish that APO would have some sort of mentor program that brought former members and current members together. Maybe someday!

I cherish you and I want you to know our memories together hold a special place in my heart. You're included in the collective experiences that make me who I am today, and I am forever grateful.

— Austin Robinson

Send   Cancel

Saturday, November 21st, 18:46

Kourtney Lee,

If you're reading this, it's because you 'liked' a Facebook post I made back in 2018. I know it's been awhile, but I'm happy to present your very own webpage and my favorite memory with you!

My favorite memory with you is when we would sit in 9th grade Health Sciences class and discuss how someday we were going to be medical professionals. I love how - in the end - NEITHER OF US ended up in the medical field LOL. How on brand of us. But I think we're both pretty happy about where we ended up in life. And in the end, that's all that matters!

I cherish you and I want you to know our memories together hold a special place in my heart. You're included in the collective experiences that make me who I am today, and I am forever grateful.

— Austin Robinson

 Send   Cancel

Saturday, November 21st, 18:48

Kristen Edwards,

If you're reading this, it's because you 'liked' a Facebook post I made back in 2018. I know it's been awhile, but I'm happy to present your very own webpage and my favorite memory with you!

Omg, I was so surprised when you liked my Facebook post because you were more of my brother's friend than mine! I remember going to high school with you, but I don't think either of us spoke to each other much. But my favorite memory with you is when you joined Key Club while I was sitting President! Regardless of how much we connected, I'm glad we did!

I cherish you and I want you to know our memories together hold a special place in my heart. You're included in the collective experiences that make me who I am today, and I am forever grateful.

— Austin Robinson

Send   Cancel

Saturday, November 21st, 18:50

Kurt Kelly,

If you're reading this, it's because you 'liked' a Facebook post I made back in 2018. I know it's been awhile, but I'm happy to present your very own webpage and my favorite memory with you!

My favorite memory with you is when we worked the Alpha Phi Omega annual blood drive together and had a deep discussion on whether or not gay people should be allowed to give blood (they should) and the rationale behind why the other side thinks the way they do. It was definitely an eye-opener to learn more about a debate that often isn't discussed at full length!

I cherish you and I want you to know our memories together hold a special place in my heart. You're included in the collective experiences that make me who I am today, and I am forever grateful.

– Austin Robinson

Send   Cancel

Saturday, November 21st, 18:52

Kyden Diaz,

If you're reading this, it's because you 'liked' a Facebook post I made back in 2018. I know it's been awhile, but I'm happy to present your very own webpage and my favorite memory with you!

YOU are one wild weirdo. We met in a time where I was pretty much experiencing a quarter-life crisis and somehow got a job at the skating rink working with middle and high school students in my hometown... at the age of 23. Enough said. Regardless of our age difference, you got me through that time in one piece. I don't think you understand the extent of that, but I thank you!

I cherish you and I want you to know our memories together hold a special place in my heart. You're included in the collective experiences that make me who I am today, and I am forever grateful.

— Austin Robinson

 Send   Cancel

Saturday, November 21st, 18:54

Kyle Walker,

If you're reading this, it's because you 'liked' a Facebook post I made back in 2018. I know it's been awhile, but I'm happy to present your very own webpage and my favorite memory with you!

Oh my gosh, my New Brunswicker queer friend. You are abso-lute-ly iconique. My favorite memory with you is living in the same province with you for a whole TWO months before finally leaving randomly. And when we became pen pals for a hot minute in either 2017 or 2018 because of my short lived pen pal program. I have such respect for the people of New Brunswick!

I cherish you and I want you to know our memories together hold a special place in my heart. You're included in the collective experiences that make me who I am today, and I am forever grateful.

— Austin Robinson

Send   Cancel

Saturday, November 21st, 18:57

Lauren Collins,

If you're reading this, it's because you 'liked' a Facebook post I made back in 2018. I know it's been awhile, but I'm happy to present your very own webpage and my favorite memory with you!

TWO SHIRTS IN ONE DAY?! Honestly, my favorite memory with you is when you were so ecstatic to receive two t-shirts in the same day. I think we should all have that kind of excitement with everything we do. I also love when we were in 7th grade and you called me to ask for the math homework set, and then I had to awkwardly remind you that we weren't even in the same math class!

I cherish you and I want you to know our memories together hold a special place in my heart. You're included in the collective experiences that make me who I am today, and I am forever grateful.

— Austin Robinson

Send   Cancel

Saturday, November 21st, 19:24

Leah Sanders,

If you're reading this, it's because you 'liked' a Facebook post I made back in 2018. I know it's been awhile, but I'm happy to present your very own webpage and my favorite memory with you!

I'm not sure who you are, but apparently we went to a HOBY seminar together, so I'm sure you're great and we had a good time! Regardless if I remember you or not, you made my time at the seminar a spectacular one and it is each and every person I met who helped me find my footing in the world with HOBY. So I thank you regardless of memory!

I cherish you and I want you to know our memories together hold a special place in my heart. You're included in the collective experiences that make me who I am today, and I am forever grateful.

— Austin Robinson

Send   Cancel

Saturday, November 21st, 19:27

Lilah Hayes,

If you're reading this, it's because you 'liked' a Facebook post I made back in 2018. I know it's been awhile, but I'm happy to present your very own webpage and my favorite memory with you!

I have been such a fan of your the second I heard your music on SoundCloud years and year ago. You were only 14 years old, and I was completely blown away by that. It's great to know that you're still making music and living your best life. You are one of the most authentic people I know, and my favorite memory with you is the connection we share through PC Music!

I cherish you and I want you to know our memories together hold a special place in my heart. You're included in the collective experiences that make me who I am today, and I am forever grateful.

– Austin Robinson

Send   Cancel

Saturday, November 21st, 19:28

Liz Shaw,

If you're reading this, it's because you 'liked' a Facebook post I made back in 2018. I know it's been awhile, but I'm happy to present your very own webpage and my favorite memory with you!

My amazing juggling friend (okay, my second amazing juggling friend) who made my time at HOBY's Advanced Leadership Academy so special. My favorite memory with you is your being the life of the party and the class clown during our time in Virginia. I don't think it could have been quite as fun without you. I just know you're spreading that fun wherever you are now!

I cherish you and I want you to know our memories together hold a special place in my heart. You're included in the collective experiences that make me who I am today, and I am forever grateful.

– Austin Robinson

 Send   Cancel

Logan Snyder,

If you're reading this, it's because you 'liked' a Facebook post I made back in 2018. I know it's been awhile, but I'm happy to present your very own webpage and my favorite memory with you!

LOGAN. I literally would never have met you if we weren't stuck on a military base in the middle of Kansas for two weeks against our will. I was surprised to discover how incredibly kind and caring you are. You were the glue that held the rest of us together when we were getting ready to kill each other. You saved us all, and we are forever grateful for that!

I cherish you and I want you to know our memories together hold a special place in my heart. You're included in the collective experiences that make me who I am today, and I am forever grateful.

— Austin Robinson

Send   Cancel

Saturday, November 21st, 19:32

Luis Dixon,

If you're reading this, it's because you 'liked' a Facebook post I made back in 2018. I know it's been awhile, but I'm happy to present your very own webpage and my favorite memory with you!

I don't know you too well at all, but it appears we have the entire UT Austin gay population as mutual friends on Facebook. So hi fellow gay! Or gay ally who is weirdly only friends with gay people? Weirder things have happened! I hope you are doing well beyond your university journey that we all collectively had together. I bet you're exactly where you need to be.

I cherish you and I want you to know our memories together hold a special place in my heart. You're included in the collective experiences that make me who I am today, and I am forever grateful.

— Austin Robinson

Send   Cancel

Saturday, November 21st, 19:35

Mackenzie Hunt,

If you're reading this, it's because you 'liked' a Facebook post I made back in 2018. I know it's been awhile, but I'm happy to present your very own webpage and my favorite memory with you!

We literally talk every day at this moment in time. We grew up in the same town and went to the same schools for 12 years, and we barely spoke once until we became coworkers in 2017. Since then, I don't think we've gone a day without talking. My favorite memory with you is being your cubicle mate in 2017 and consistently getting in trouble for "talking too much" (doesn't exist)!

I cherish you and I want you to know our memories together hold a special place in my heart. You're included in the collective experiences that make me who I am today, and I am forever grateful.

— Austin Robinson

 Send Cancel

Saturday, November 21st, 19:37

Maria Holmes,

If you're reading this, it's because you 'liked' a Facebook post I made back in 2018. I know it's been awhile, but I'm happy to present your very own webpage and my favorite memory with you!

Coding queen! You were part of that Computer Science fraternity that I tried to infiltrate despite being an English major who didn't even know what a computer was. You'd be so proud of me now - I coded the website this webpage is on! My favorite memory with you is how supportive you were about me trying get into your organization that clearly wasn't for me!

I cherish you and I want you to know our memories together hold a special place in my heart. You're included in the collective experiences that make me who I am today, and I am forever grateful.

– Austin Robinson

Send   Cancel

Saturday, November 21st, 19:39

Marshall Black,

If you're reading this, it's because you 'liked' a Facebook post I made back in 2018. I know it's been awhile, but I'm happy to present your very own webpage and my favorite memory with you!

Omg, you've been Instagram messaging me as I've been building this project. I'm glad we still keep in touch, even if it isn't as often as I would like. The friendship triangle I have with you and Connor is so special to me. And the fact that you now work with one of my old childhood friends! My favorite memory with you is you letting me and Connor continually use your face for our books!

I cherish you and I want you to know our memories together hold a special place in my heart. You're included in the collective experiences that make me who I am today, and I am forever grateful.

— Austin Robinson

 Send   Cancel

Saturday, November 21st, 19:41

Mary Palmer,

If you're reading this, it's because you 'liked' a Facebook post I made back in 2018. I know it's been awhile, but I'm happy to present your very own webpage and my favorite memory with you!

My favorite memory with you is seeing your smile every week in the Alpha Phi Omega meetings! You were ALWAYS smiling, and that made the rest of us smile, no matter how gloomy the day was. You also held the organization on your shoulders and assured it was a great time for all of us involved. I thank you for making my university experience one of the best!

I cherish you and I want you to know our memories together hold a special place in my heart. You're included in the collective experiences that make me who I am today, and I am forever grateful.

– Austin Robinson

 Send   Cancel

Saturday, November 21st, 19:43

Matthew Rose,

If you're reading this, it's because you 'liked' a Facebook post I made back in 2018. I know it's been awhile, but I'm happy to present your very own webpage and my favorite memory with you!

I am continually surprised by you. I remember you being this macho guy who exuded masculinity like so many other Texas Blazers, but now I see you posting pretty far-left leaning social commentary on Facebook and I just never expect it! I love it. My favorite memory with you is just chatting with you in the meetings, as I always found you pretty interesting!

I cherish you and I want you to know our memories together hold a special place in my heart. You're included in the collective experiences that make me who I am today, and I am forever grateful.

— Austin Robinson

 Send   Cancel

Saturday, November 21st, 19:45

Matthew Stone,

If you're reading this, it's because you 'liked' a Facebook post I made back in 2018. I know it's been awhile, but I'm happy to present your very own webpage and my favorite memory with you!

I am so sorry I never responded to your message in 2018 when I promised I would, and for not publishing this book sooner when you expressed how excited you are for it. My favorite memory is how vocally supportive you were of my brand. You said it proved that anyone could make anything real with just some hard work. That means the world to me!

I cherish you and I want you to know our memories together hold a special place in my heart. You're included in the collective experiences that make me who I am today, and I am forever grateful.

– Austin Robinson

Send   Cancel

Saturday, November 21st, 19:47

Maximus Salazar,

If you're reading this, it's because you 'liked' a Facebook post I made back in 2018. I know it's been awhile, but I'm happy to present your very own webpage and my favorite memory with you!

My favorite memory with you is when you supported mine and Daniel's bid for Student Body President and Vice Present at UT Austin! I believe you were part of the satirical paper Texas Travesty, which was a huge supporter of us (although not officially). It meant the world to us, even though we were running as a joke. Thank you for letting us joke!

I cherish you and I want you to know our memories together hold a special place in my heart. You're included in the collective experiences that make me who I am today, and I am forever grateful.

— Austin Robinson

 Send Cancel

Saturday, November 21st, 19:51

Megan Garza,

If you're reading this, it's because you 'liked' a Facebook post I made back in 2018. I know it's been awhile, but I'm happy to present your very own webpage and my favorite memory with you!

I'VE BEEN WAITING FOR THIS ONE. My favorite memory with you is when you asked the server at The Cheesecake Factory for 3 things of ranch and he brought you THREE GRAVY BOATS FILLED WITH RANCH. I truly cannot believe that happened, and it is also my favorite memory in the history of The Cheesecake Factory. So thanks!

I cherish you and I want you to know our memories together hold a special place in my heart. You're included in the collective experiences that make me who I am today, and I am forever grateful.

— Austin Robinson

Send   Cancel

Saturday, November 21st, 19:53

Megan Daniels,

If you're reading this, it's because you 'liked' a Facebook post I made back in 2018. I know it's been awhile, but I'm happy to present your very own webpage and my favorite memory with you!

My favorite memory with you is when you were the Key Club Texas-Oklahoma District Governor. Honestly, that pretty much didn't involve me (although I did vote for you), but I just respected you for being in that position so much. Especially as a high school student. I definitely could've never done that - which is why I dropped out of the District Treasurer race!

I cherish you and I want you to know our memories together hold a special place in my heart. You're included in the collective experiences that make me who I am today, and I am forever grateful.

— Austin Robinson

Send   Cancel

Saturday, November 21st, 19:54

Megha Nichols,

If you're reading this, it's because you 'liked' a Facebook post I made back in 2018. I know it's been awhile, but I'm happy to present your very own webpage and my favorite memory with you!

My favorite memory with you is when we had a very long conversation on the phone about how you write down all of your friends in a calendar and plan a time to check in with them every single month. I felt that was so powerful. And although we didn't end up keeping that promise to each other, I just know you're taking care of the best friends in your life right now!

I cherish you and I want you to know our memories together hold a special place in my heart. You're included in the collective experiences that make me who I am today, and I am forever grateful.

– Austin Robinson

Send   Cancel

Mia Stephens,

If you're reading this, it's because you 'liked' a Facebook post I made back in 2018. I know it's been awhile, but I'm happy to present your very own webpage and my favorite memory with you!

My favorite memory with you is how caring you were to all of the patrons of the skating rink while we were working. It was so odd that I was 23 years old and that all of my coworkers were middle and high school students, but you didn't let me feel ashamed for that. Even at such a young age, you knew how to be kind to every person you came into contact with!

I cherish you and I want you to know our memories together hold a special place in my heart. You're included in the collective experiences that make me who I am today, and I am forever grateful.

— Austin Robinson

Send   Cancel

Saturday, November 21st, 19:57

Michael Soto,

If you're reading this, it's because you 'liked' a Facebook post I made back in 2018. I know it's been awhile, but I'm happy to present your very own webpage and my favorite memory with you!

I miss you so much, my Colorado friend. I had so much fun with you and Steven when we would spend time together at Alpha Phi Omega events. My favorite memory with you is when we used Yik Yak at the APO National Convention to just spam "Smegg ma" and everyone talked about it throughout the convention and also asked that we shut up!

I cherish you and I want you to know our memories together hold a special place in my heart. You're included in the collective experiences that make me who I am today, and I am forever grateful.

– Austin Robinson

Send   Cancel

Saturday, November 21st, 20:01

Michael Dunn,

If you're reading this, it's because you 'liked' a Facebook post I made back in 2018. I know it's been awhile, but I'm happy to present your very own webpage and my favorite memory with you!

My favorite memory with you is when we basically dated while I casually "lived" in Los Angeles for a hot two months. And then your ex - who I didn't know was your ex, but was also one of my good friends - got extremely mad at both of us. And then we sort of just never talked again until you asked me to edit your sci-fi novel. Which is honestly how most relationships SHOULD go!

I cherish you and I want you to know our memories together hold a special place in my heart. You're included in the collective experiences that make me who I am today, and I am forever grateful.

— Austin Robinson

    Send   Cancel   128

Saturday, November 21st, 20:03

Muata Gardner,

If you're reading this, it's because you 'liked' a Facebook post I made back in 2018. I know it's been awhile, but I'm happy to present your very own webpage and my favorite memory with you!

My favorite memory with you is when me, you, and Kate would sing Mercy by Kanye West in the back of our Economics class at Stanford University, and absolutely everyone would want us to be doing literally anything else. But at the same time, you were so passionate about JSA, an organization I had only just gotten acquainted with. But I'm so glad I did!

I cherish you and I want you to know our memories together hold a special place in my heart. You're included in the collective experiences that make me who I am today, and I am forever grateful.

— Austin Robinson

Send   Cancel

Saturday, November 21st, 20:06

Murray Weaver,

If you're reading this, it's because you 'liked' a Facebook post I made back in 2018. I know it's been awhile, but I'm happy to present your very own webpage and my favorite memory with you!

My favorite memory with you is when we met up at your university in Boston for a hot five minutes. The best five minutes of my life, tbh. I've followed your journey with music and art, and I am incredibly proud of where you are now. I wish I had the courage you have to just go out and create these beautiful pieces of art. All I can do is sell t-shirts with my name on them!

I cherish you and I want you to know our memories together hold a special place in my heart. You're included in the collective experiences that make me who I am today, and I am forever grateful.

— Austin Robinson

 Send   Cancel

Saturday, November 21st, 20:07

Myra Vazquez,

If you're reading this, it's because you 'liked' a Facebook post I made back in 2018. I know it's been awhile, but I'm happy to present your very own webpage and my favorite memory with you!

I am actually so surprised that you liked my post. You are my ex-boyfriend's best friend and we never really hung out. Like, at all. Like, I don't know anything about you. But I guess I can say that you're beautiful and I'm glad that I know of your existence. And you've made the lives of other people in my life better, so I thank you eternally for that. Keep being you!

I cherish you and I want you to know our memories together hold a special place in my heart. You're included in the collective experiences that make me who I am today, and I am forever grateful.

— Austin Robinson

Send   Cancel

Saturday, November 21st, 20:09

Natalie Santos,

If you're reading this, it's because you 'liked' a Facebook post I made back in 2018. I know it's been awhile, but I'm happy to present your very own webpage and my favorite memory with you!

My favorite memory with you is how involved you were with Student Government at UT Austin. I hold high respect for anyone trying to make the lives of their fellow students better. And you encapsulated that. I know we don't talk anymore, but I truly hope that you're living life with the same passion you had for making others as happy as they can be!

I cherish you and I want you to know our memories together hold a special place in my heart. You're included in the collective experiences that make me who I am today, and I am forever grateful.

— Austin Robinson

 Send   Cancel

Saturday, November 21st, 20:12

Nathan Hansen,

If you're reading this, it's because you 'liked' a Facebook post I made back in 2018. I know it's been awhile, but I'm happy to present your very own webpage and my favorite memory with you!

My favorite memory with you is how you were best friends with my best friends, but we never spoke because we had a gay friend competition (basically we were each other's nemeses), or maybe it was sexual tension. Who knows, but it was great and I'm glad I got to experience that rare occasion with you. And now you're out there making the world a better place!

I cherish you and I want you to know our memories together hold a special place in my heart. You're included in the collective experiences that make me who I am today, and I am forever grateful.

- Austin Robinson

Send   Cancel

Saturday, November 21st, 20:14

Nicholas Cunningham,

If you're reading this, it's because you 'liked' a Facebook post I made back in 2018. I know it's been awhile, but I'm happy to present your very own webpage and my favorite memory with you!

My sweet, sweet University Democrats boy. You were the reason I kept thinking about joining that organization! I'm not entirely sure why I never fully joined it. But regardless, y'all (and you, especially) backed mine and Daniel's bid for Student Body President and Vice President. You were alway so supportive of not only that endeavor, but also every AJR project I had!

I cherish you and I want you to know our memories together hold a special place in my heart. You're included in the collective experiences that make me who I am today, and I am forever grateful.

— Austin Robinson

 Send   Cancel

Saturday, November 21st, 21:30

Nick Elliot,

If you're reading this, it's because you 'liked' a Facebook post I made back in 2018. I know it's been awhile, but I'm happy to present your very own webpage and my favorite memory with you!

My number one juggling friend (I already made the webpage for my other juggling friend, so I have to clarify). My favorite memory with you is when I visited you at your university in Tulsa, Oklahoma and we got breakfast at a local diner that was honestly incredible. I'm so glad we met at HOBY Arkansas that one time I went forever ago. I hope you're doing well!

I cherish you and I want you to know our memories together hold a special place in my heart. You're included in the collective experiences that make me who I am today, and I am forever grateful.

– Austin Robinson

Send   Cancel

Saturday, November 21st, 21:33

Nick Lane,

If you're reading this, it's because you 'liked' a Facebook post I made back in 2018. I know it's been awhile, but I'm happy to present your very own webpage and my favorite memory with you!

I'm not entirely sure who you are, but it looks like we're fellow Alpha Phi Omega members (or were, I guess - university is over!). I hope you had as good of a time as I did in the organization. It looks like you did, from the pictures of the past. Sometimes I have to look through people's Facebook profiles in order to write them a proper webpage - which makes me feel like a stalker!

I cherish you and I want you to know our memories together hold a special place in my heart. You're included in the collective experiences that make me who I am today, and I am forever grateful.

- Austin Robinson

Send   Cancel

Saturday, November 21st, 21:35

Niki Riley,

If you're reading this, it's because you 'liked' a Facebook post I made back in 2018. I know it's been awhile, but I'm happy to present your very own webpage and my favorite memory with you!

A fellow JSA Stanford University alum! I had so much fun those five weeks we spent on Stanford's campus. It was tough, but it was worth it for all of the friendships I gained throughout the time - especially yours! It's wild to think that you're married with a child now. I'm not sure many of the others (including me) can claim those accomplishments. I hope it's going well!

I cherish you and I want you to know our memories together hold a special place in my heart. You're included in the collective experiences that make me who I am today, and I am forever grateful.

— Austin Robinson

Send   Cancel

Saturday, November 21st, 21:38

Noel Alvarado,

If you're reading this, it's because you 'liked' a Facebook post I made back in 2018. I know it's been awhile, but I'm happy to present your very own webpage and my favorite memory with you!

My little raccoon. I'll never forget the time we spent in Los Angeles together. I know that I didn't act my best on our first date, but boy did we have fun. It was one of the first times I had ever been drunk, and my FIRST time throwing up because of drinking. I woke up the next morning with the business card of a major music label executive in my pocket!

I cherish you and I want you to know our memories together hold a special place in my heart. You're included in the collective experiences that make me who I am today, and I am forever grateful.

— Austin Robinson

Send   Cancel

Saturday, November 21st, 21:40

Olivia Carroll,

If you're reading this, it's because you 'liked' a Facebook post I made back in 2018. I know it's been awhile, but I'm happy to present your very own webpage and my favorite memory with you!

My favorite memory with you is when you were dating my best friend and we would all hang out together and play video games. You are probably the only person I've ever met who knows who Alan Resnick is, and I loved that so much. We have such similar senses of humor, which is rare to find. I also love how true you are to yourself. I know you're making sure you're happy!

I cherish you and I want you to know our memories together hold a special place in my heart. You're included in the collective experiences that make me who I am today, and I am forever grateful.

– Austin Robinson

Send   Cancel

Saturday, November 21st, 21:43

Parker Carpenter,

If you're reading this, it's because you 'liked' a Facebook post I made back in 2018. I know it's been awhile, but I'm happy to present your very own webpage and my favorite memory with you!

My favorite memory with you is when you bought an AUSTIN JAMES ROBINSON t-shirt and I had to secretly drop it off on your door step because your mother hates gay people and thought I was trying to have sex with you. Also, I love that you started your own t-shirt brand inspired by mine, and that people actually bought your products!

I cherish you and I want you to know our memories together hold a special place in my heart. You're included in the collective experiences that make me who I am today, and I am forever grateful.

— Austin Robinson

Send   Cancel

Saturday, November 21st, 21:48

Parsa Rios,

If you're reading this, it's because you 'liked' a Facebook post I made back in 2018. I know it's been awhile, but I'm happy to present your very own webpage and my favorite memory with you!

You are one of the sweetest people alive! My favorite memory with you is when you invited me to your United States Citizen Naturalization ceremony. It was great to hang out with you and your family for a couple of hours while we waited for the ceremony to start. It's the only one I've attended, but I'm attending another one soon for my significant other!

I cherish you and I want you to know our memories together hold a special place in my heart. You're included in the collective experiences that make me who I am today, and I am forever grateful.

– Austin Robinson

Send   Cancel

Saturday, November 21st, 21:50

Patrick Goldman,

If you're reading this, it's because you 'liked' a Facebook post I made back in 2018. I know it's been awhile, but I'm happy to present your very own webpage and my favorite memory with you!

You're so special to me that your name remains the only one unchanged in this project. No anonymity for you! My favorite memory with you has to be when we bought inflatable tubes, aired them up at a sketchy gas station, and then rode them on the river when we legally weren't allowed to do so. And the fact that you basically saved our lives that night!

I cherish you and I want you to know our memories together hold a special place in my heart. You're included in the collective experiences that make me who I am today, and I am forever grateful.

— Austin Robinson

Send   **Cancel**

Saturday, November 21st, 21:52

Patrick Harper,

If you're reading this, it's because you 'liked' a Facebook post I made back in 2018. I know it's been awhile, but I'm happy to present your very own webpage and my favorite memory with you!

You are a fitness LEGEND. I'm truly in awe of not only your body, but also the fact that you created an entire brand around it and are doing incredibly well for yourself because of it. I am consistently inspired by you when I see your social media posts, and you keep me energized to finish my passion projects. I sincerely hope your dreams never stop growing!

I cherish you and I want you to know our memories together hold a special place in my heart. You're included in the collective experiences that make me who I am today, and I am forever grateful.

— Austin Robinson

Send   Cancel

Saturday, November 21st, 21:54

Pedro Wheeler,

If you're reading this, it's because you 'liked' a Facebook post I made back in 2018. I know it's been awhile, but I'm happy to present your very own webpage and my favorite memory with you!

My favorite memory with you is when me and Skyla went on a double date with you and your boyfriend at the time. We attended the Texas Blazers' Yacht Night or whatever the hell it was called. Basically we were drunk on a boat for way too long with a bunch of people in suits. But you made that bearable, and I had such a great night getting to know you!

I cherish you and I want you to know our memories together hold a special place in my heart. You're included in the collective experiences that make me who I am today, and I am forever grateful.

– Austin Robinson

 Send   Cancel

Saturday, November 21st, 21:57

Rob Carr,

If you're reading this, it's because you 'liked' a Facebook post I made back in 2018. I know it's been awhile, but I'm happy to present your very own webpage and my favorite memory with you!

My favorite memory with you is when you and Kyra let me crash on your couch the night before I drove halfway across the country just to get on a plane to The Netherlands for absolutely no reason and with no plan. Oh wait, I also LOVE that you and Kyra did the campaign photos for my energy drink: AJR H2O. That will forever go down as one of my favorite things!

I cherish you and I want you to know our memories together hold a special place in my heart. You're included in the collective experiences that make me who I am today, and I am forever grateful.

— Austin Robinson

 Send **Cancel**

Saturday, November 21st, 21:59

Ryan Jacobs,

If you're reading this, it's because you 'liked' a Facebook post I made back in 2018. I know it's been awhile, but I'm happy to present your very own webpage and my favorite memory with you!

My wonderful New Brunswicker turned Haligonian. I'm so happy you came back to Saint John for the Fundy Fringe Festival and that I got to meet you and get exclusive seats to your play/musical. I also loved attending the Canadian version of HAMILTON with you. And I got to visit you in Halifax two years later, as well as your boyfriend and your friends!

I cherish you and I want you to know our memories together hold a special place in my heart. You're included in the collective experiences that make me who I am today, and I am forever grateful.

– Austin Robinson

Send   **Cancel**

Saturday, November 21st, 22:02

Ryan Singh,

If you're reading this, it's because you 'liked' a Facebook post I made back in 2018. I know it's been awhile, but I'm happy to present your very own webpage and my favorite memory with you!

RYAN. You are still one of my best friends to this day. You are the reason I found housing in Portland so fast when I moved. You are the reason I started my web development journey. You are the reason I am who I am today! My favorite memory with you is pranking you by lying naked in your bed and then being forced to wash your sheets because you hated that!

I cherish you and I want you to know our memories together hold a special place in my heart. You're included in the collective experiences that make me who I am today, and I am forever grateful.

– Austin Robinson

Send   Cancel

Saturday, November 21st, 22:09

Ryan Austin,

If you're reading this, it's because you 'liked' a Facebook post I made back in 2018. I know it's been awhile, but I'm happy to present your very own webpage and my favorite memory with you!

My favorite memory with you is hanging out with you at all of the Texas Blazers events they put on, and realizing that we felt like we were in more of a service organization than a social one. I always appreciated the fact that you joined the organization to help others, opposed to helping yourself. I really hope you're still spending your time helping others!

I cherish you and I want you to know our memories together hold a special place in my heart. You're included in the collective experiences that make me who I am today, and I am forever grateful.

— Austin Robinson

 Send **Cancel**

Saturday, November 21st, 22:11

Sailesh Franklin,

If you're reading this, it's because you 'liked' a Facebook post I made back in 2018. I know it's been awhile, but I'm happy to present your very own webpage and my favorite memory with you!

You already know I have to say my favorite memory with you is when we met at the Texas State Student Alliance conference in 2011. Who knew that a couple years later, we would be entering the same university and eventually the same student organization. We became incredibly close in university, and I'm glad to know I'll always have a friend in you!

I cherish you and I want you to know our memories together hold a special place in my heart. You're included in the collective experiences that make me who I am today, and I am forever grateful.

— Austin Robinson

Send   Cancel

Saturday, November 21st, 22:14

Samantha Larson,

If you're reading this, it's because you 'liked' a Facebook post I made back in 2018. I know it's been awhile, but I'm happy to present your very own webpage and my favorite memory with you!

My favorite memory with you is when you would wear my AUSTIN JAMES ROBINSON t-shirt to every HOBY event you could. You were quite possibly my biggest APO support, which meant a lot to me because I never thought more of my t-shirts than just that: t-shirts. You and all the others made them into something more meaningful. Thank you!

I cherish you and I want you to know our memories together hold a special place in my heart. You're included in the collective experiences that make me who I am today, and I am forever grateful.

— Austin Robinson

Send   **Cancel**

Saturday, November 21st, 22:17

Samuel Burke,

If you're reading this, it's because you 'liked' a Facebook post I made back in 2018. I know it's been awhile, but I'm happy to present your very own webpage and my favorite memory with you!

My favorite memory with you is meeting you at a UT Liberal Arts event that I was giving a presentation at and then later on finding out that you had also joined Alpha Phi Omega. You ended up being one of the best serving volunteers the new APO class had, and I respected that so much. I really hope you're still going out and changing the world for the better!

I cherish you and I want you to know our memories together hold a special place in my heart. You're included in the collective experiences that make me who I am today, and I am forever grateful.

— Austin Robinson

Send   Cancel

Saturday, November 21st, 22:23

Samuel Harvey,

If you're reading this, it's because you 'liked' a Facebook post I made back in 2018. I know it's been awhile, but I'm happy to present your very own webpage and my favorite memory with you!

My favorite memory with you is when we went to Blazer Tag with Alpha Phi Omega and I got to know you better and take pictures with stuffed minions. You were pretty popular in the organization because you were known for being a welcoming person who liked having conversations with others. I know you're still doing that in your adult life!

I cherish you and I want you to know our memories together hold a special place in my heart. You're included in the collective experiences that make me who I am today, and I am forever grateful.

— Austin Robinson

Send　　**Cancel**

Saturday, November 21st, 22:25

Santiago Espinoza,

If you're reading this, it's because you 'liked' a Facebook post I made back in 2018. I know it's been awhile, but I'm happy to present your very own webpage and my favorite memory with you!

My favorite memory with you is when I was taking the UT Austin McComb's School of Business Foundation courses and you tried to teach me Microsoft Excel. I was in a course that was just entirely Excel, and you wouldn't let me fail! Although I ended up dropping out, it meant the world to me that you wanted to help me succeed in something that you were passionate about!

I cherish you and I want you to know our memories together hold a special place in my heart. You're included in the collective experiences that make me who I am today, and I am forever grateful.

– Austin Robinson

Send   Cancel

Saturday, November 21st, 22:27

Sasha Bishop,

If you're reading this, it's because you 'liked' a Facebook post I made back in 2018. I know it's been awhile, but I'm happy to present your very own webpage and my favorite memory with you!

I never knew you that well, but I do remember that you were part of one of the sister organizations to Texas Blazers! We have a ton of mutual friends in both organizations, so I know we've crossed paths once or twice. I apologize for not having a favorite memory, but I know you must be making the world happier and doing all you can to achieve your dreams!

I cherish you and I want you to know our memories together hold a special place in my heart. You're included in the collective experiences that make me who I am today, and I am forever grateful.

— Austin Robinson

Send **Cancel**

Saturday, November 21st, 22:35

Sean Vega,

If you're reading this, it's because you 'liked' a Facebook post I made back in 2018. I know it's been awhile, but I'm happy to present your very own webpage and my favorite memory with you!

I am trying to pinpoint exactly when we met - I know it was at a Kiwanis K-Family event, but I'm not sure if it was Key Club or Circle Key. I wanna say it was at that Circle K leadership conference in Indianapolis. Regardless, my favorite memory with you is talking about you getting your pilot's license and going on all of these adventures in the sky!

I cherish you and I want you to know our memories together hold a special place in my heart. You're included in the collective experiences that make me who I am today, and I am forever grateful.

— Austin Robinson

Send   Cancel

Saturday, November 21st, 22:39

Seth Lynch,

If you're reading this, it's because you 'liked' a Facebook post I made back in 2018. I know it's been awhile, but I'm happy to present your very own webpage and my favorite memory with you!

My favorite memory with you is meeting you on a gay dating app on my way to the Circle K International Convention in Tennessee. Who knew we would become such close friends and I would eventually visit you again in a Memphis bar years later. I also loved that you taught me about Bucksnort, Tennessee - I think about it quite literally all of the time!

I cherish you and I want you to know our memories together hold a special place in my heart. You're included in the collective experiences that make me who I am today, and I am forever grateful.

— Austin Robinson

Send   Cancel

Saturday, November 21st, 22:43

Shannon Reid,

If you're reading this, it's because you 'liked' a Facebook post I made back in 2018. I know it's been awhile, but I'm happy to present your very own webpage and my favorite memory with you!

I have a favorite memory OF you and a favorite memory WITH you. My favorite memory of you is when you and your best friend made the funniest YouTube channel I have ever seen, and my favorite memory with you is when I saw you in our hometown's Goodwill and I pretended like I was your biggest fan thanks to your YouTube channel. Overall, you're hilarious!

I cherish you and I want you to know our memories together hold a special place in my heart. You're included in the collective experiences that make me who I am today, and I am forever grateful.

— Austin Robinson

Send   Cancel

Saturday, November 21st, 22:46

Sheila Fuller,

If you're reading this, it's because you 'liked' a Facebook post I made back in 2018. I know it's been awhile, but I'm happy to present your very own webpage and my favorite memory with you!

My favorite memory with you is when I was staying in Halifax and you decided to give me a call to ask my advice and give me advice. You told me about how your job in Kansas City was paying for your masters degree, but you weren't sure how much you enjoyed the work. I'm glad that you're now living back in Austin and at a company that I hope you are happier at!

I cherish you and I want you to know our memories together hold a special place in my heart. You're included in the collective experiences that make me who I am today, and I am forever grateful.

— Austin Robinson

Send   Cancel

Saturday, November 21st, 22:48

Spencer Weber,

If you're reading this, it's because you 'liked' a Facebook post I made back in 2018. I know it's been awhile, but I'm happy to present your very own webpage and my favorite memory with you!

My beautiful, beautiful Spencer. You are living your life to your fullest in Los Angeles! Where you belong and where you deserve to be. My favorite memory with you is visiting you in Los Angeles and going to a house dinner with your friend and the creator of The Oblongs, which I grew up watching as a child. You always believed in me when I "lived" in LA!

I cherish you and I want you to know our memories together hold a special place in my heart. You're included in the collective experiences that make me who I am today, and I am forever grateful.

— Austin Robinson

Send   Cancel

Saturday, November 21st, 22:53

Spencer Fields,

If you're reading this, it's because you 'liked' a Facebook post I made back in 2018. I know it's been awhile, but I'm happy to present your very own webpage and my favorite memory with you!

My favorite memory with you is viewing all of your social media posts and realizing how beautiful they are. You are an amazing photographer and photo manipulator. I'm also obsessed with your mustache and how much you look like a model. I'm glad we have similar tastes in art and music. Never stop being different, and never stop being yourself!

I cherish you and I want you to know our memories together hold a special place in my heart. You're included in the collective experiences that make me who I am today, and I am forever grateful.

— Austin Robinson

 Send   Cancel

Saturday, November 21st, 22:55

Stella Little,

If you're reading this, it's because you 'liked' a Facebook post I made back in 2018. I know it's been awhile, but I'm happy to present your very own webpage and my favorite memory with you!

My favorite memory with you is how much we clicked while we were both in Alpha Phi Omega. You were ALMOST my Little (the fact that my name generator gave you that as a last name is completely coincidental), which would have been fun! I also love that you gave me web development advice when I was going through a career crisis and wanted to know more about CS!

I cherish you and I want you to know our memories together hold a special place in my heart. You're included in the collective experiences that make me who I am today, and I am forever grateful.

— Austin Robinson

Send   Cancel

Saturday, November 21st, 22:57

Steven Day,

If you're reading this, it's because you 'liked' a Facebook post I made back in 2018. I know it's been awhile, but I'm happy to present your very own webpage and my favorite memory with you!

My favorite memory with you is when we kissed at a mall in Chicago during the Alpha Phi Omega National Convention. It was a total dare, but you were up for it. Then we went on to spam Yik Yak and make all of the attendees and hotel guests mad at us (but they never figured out it was us!). You were always one of my favorite people, and I'm sad we don't talk more nowadays!

I cherish you and I want you to know our memories together hold a special place in my heart. You're included in the collective experiences that make me who I am today, and I am forever grateful.

— Austin Robinson

Send   **Cancel**

Saturday, November 21st, 23:00

Stewart Bowman,

If you're reading this, it's because you 'liked' a Facebook post I made back in 2018. I know it's been awhile, but I'm happy to present your very own webpage and my favorite memory with you!

My favorite memory with you is driving 8 hours to visit our good friend Seth. We listened to a lot of music that we both liked and shared the worst jokes imaginable. We started that joke twitter account that literally gained NO traction. I don't even remember what we decided to call our comedy duo name. It's probably for the best that we're not trying to further our comedy careers!

I cherish you and I want you to know our memories together hold a special place in my heart. You're included in the collective experiences that make me who I am today, and I am forever grateful.

– Austin Robinson

Send   Cancel

Saturday, November 21st, 23:02

Suhas Schultz,

If you're reading this, it's because you 'liked' a Facebook post I made back in 2018. I know it's been awhile, but I'm happy to present your very own webpage and my favorite memory with you!

My favorite memory with you is how close you were with so many Texas Blazers. You would have done anything for us. You made the most out of that organization, and I believe you got a lot out of it. You made it what it was, and I thank you for that. I know we didn't hang out much, but I also know you're following your dreams and having the best time of your life!

I cherish you and I want you to know our memories together hold a special place in my heart. You're included in the collective experiences that make me who I am today, and I am forever grateful.

— Austin Robinson

Send　　**Cancel**

Sunday, November 22nd, 09:55

Tee Fowler,

If you're reading this, it's because you 'liked' a Facebook post I made back in 2018. I know it's been awhile, but I'm happy to present your very own webpage and my favorite memory with you!

I have never heard of you before, you're not on my Facebook as a friend, and I don't know what's going on! Maybe you were one of those bots that sometimes likes posts for no reason? I get a lot of fake sexy women bots who use the laugh react when I post serious things - it's truly so odd. Or maybe pathetic. Who knows? Anyway, whether you're real or not, have a good day!

I cherish you and I want you to know our memories together hold a special place in my heart. You're included in the collective experiences that make me who I am today, and I am forever grateful.

— Austin Robinson

 Send Cancel

Sunday, November 22nd, 09:57

Terence Brewer,

If you're reading this, it's because you 'liked' a Facebook post I made back in 2018. I know it's been awhile, but I'm happy to present your very own webpage and my favorite memory with you!

My favorite memory with you is how completely unique and true to yourself you were while we were in Alpha Phi Omega and on UT's campus. You had your own style, you were fashionable, and you weren't afraid to be judged for it by anyone. I think most of us thought you were pretty cool. Keep being your own breed of greatness, as I'm sure you're still doing!

I cherish you and I want you to know our memories together hold a special place in my heart. You're included in the collective experiences that make me who I am today, and I am forever grateful.

— Austin Robinson

Send   **Cancel**

Sunday, November 22nd, 09:58

Teresa May,

If you're reading this, it's because you 'liked' a Facebook post I made back in 2018. I know it's been awhile, but I'm happy to present your very own webpage and my favorite memory with you!

My favorite memory with you is when we attended the HOBY Texas North seminar together all the way back in 2011! And then I ended up going to the same university as you (UT Austin), although I think you basically graduated as soon as I entered. Rude! JK. I hope everything is going well for you in Philadelphia. I hear they have amazing HOBY seminars over in Pennsylvania!

I cherish you and I want you to know our memories together hold a special place in my heart. You're included in the collective experiences that make me who I am today, and I am forever grateful.

— Austin Robinson

Send   Cancel

Sunday, November 22nd, 10:02

Theresa Coldwell,

If you're reading this, it's because you 'liked' a Facebook post I made back in 2018. I know it's been awhile, but I'm happy to present your very own webpage and my favorite memory with you!

My favorite memory with you is when we were in Alpha Phi Omega together and did a ton of volunteer work! I believe we did an extra long shift at one of the APO annual Blood Drives together. I always admired your passion for helping others and knew that you joined APO for the right reasons. I hope you're doing well wherever you are!

I cherish you and I want you to know our memories together hold a special place in my heart. You're included in the collective experiences that make me who I am today, and I am forever grateful.

– Austin Robinson

Send   Cancel

Sunday, November 22nd, 10:07

Toni Miranda,

If you're reading this, it's because you 'liked' a Facebook post I made back in 2018. I know it's been awhile, but I'm happy to present your very own webpage and my favorite memory with you!

I guess we really only have one memory together, and it's when I came to visit you, Jonathan, and Ethan in Pittsburg. I honestly can't remember why I was even in the area, but it was great getting to meet that part of the family and be in Pittsburg for the first time ever. Thank you for having me over, and I hope I get to see y'all in person again someday soon!

I cherish you and I want you to know our memories together hold a special place in my heart. You're included in the collective experiences that make me who I am today, and I am forever grateful.

— Austin Robinson

Send   Cancel

Sunday, November 22nd, 10:09

Tony Craig,

If you're reading this, it's because you 'liked' a Facebook post I made back in 2018. I know it's been awhile, but I'm happy to present your very own webpage and my favorite memory with you!

My beautiful APO Little, Tony. I am so happy that we were all so close while part of that organization. My favorite memory with you is hanging out in yours and Ryan's apartment and discussing aspirations, job prospects, and goals. I'm so jealous that you and Ryan got to work and live together. I wish I could have joined along. Maybe someday that'll happen!

I cherish you and I want you to know our memories together hold a special place in my heart. You're included in the collective experiences that make me who I am today, and I am forever grateful.

— Austin Robinson

 Send   **Cancel**

Sunday, November 22nd, 10:12

Torii Lowe,

If you're reading this, it's because you 'liked' a Facebook post I made back in 2018. I know it's been awhile, but I'm happy to present your very own webpage and my favorite memory with you!

You already know my favorite memory with you is when you asked me to officiate your wedding and make it an AUSTIN JAMES ROBINSON theme. We wore our AJR t-shirts and had it with your whole family. I bet they were like... okay, WHAT is going on. I know y'all divorced a year later, which was probably my brand's fault TBH (a curse), but thank you for that memory!

I cherish you and I want you to know our memories together hold a special place in my heart. You're included in the collective experiences that make me who I am today, and I am forever grateful.

— Austin Robinson

Send   Cancel

Sunday, November 22nd, 10:14

Travis Leonard,

If you're reading this, it's because you 'liked' a Facebook post I made back in 2018. I know it's been awhile, but I'm happy to present your very own webpage and my favorite memory with you!

I have SO many favorite memories with you, so this is going to be hard. But I would say my favorite memories with you consist of mountains. The first is when you took me up to the top of an Alaskan mountain in Anchorage, and the second is when we got stuck on the top of Mt. Hood. Anyway, let's literally never have another memory with each other that doesn't involve mountains!

I cherish you and I want you to know our memories together hold a special place in my heart. You're included in the collective experiences that make me who I am today, and I am forever grateful.

– Austin Robinson

Send   **Cancel**

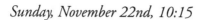

Sunday, November 22nd, 10:15

Trent Gregory,

If you're reading this, it's because you 'liked' a Facebook post I made back in 2018. I know it's been awhile, but I'm happy to present your very own webpage and my favorite memory with you!

My favorite memory with you is when I had just started drinking alcohol at the age of 22 and you invited me over for a party. Naturally I got black-out drunk because I didn't have years of knowing what my limit was. I cannot remember much about that night, but I know we had an amazing time and that is was memorable for pretty much everyone else!

I cherish you and I want you to know our memories together hold a special place in my heart. You're included in the collective experiences that make me who I am today, and I am forever grateful.

— Austin Robinson

Send   Cancel

Sunday, November 22nd, 11:32

Tyler Love,

If you're reading this, it's because you 'liked' a Facebook post I made back in 2018. I know it's been awhile, but I'm happy to present your very own webpage and my favorite memory with you!

Omg, you literally have a shout-out at the beginning of this book! My favorite memory with you is going to Halloweentown in St. Helens, Oregon and seeing the parade and the square. Also, that time that we ate pizza with green apple slices on it in Redwood City, California. Wait, also that time we ate DQ on the floor of my small studio apartment & watched Over The Garden Wall!

I cherish you and I want you to know our memories together hold a special place in my heart. You're included in the collective experiences that make me who I am today, and I am forever grateful.

— Austin Robinson

Send **Cancel**

Sunday, November 22nd, 11:41

Tyler Cervantes,

If you're reading this, it's because you 'liked' a Facebook post I made back in 2018. I know it's been awhile, but I'm happy to present your very own webpage and my favorite memory with you!

Omg, you literally have a shout-out at the beginning of this book! My favorite memory with you is how much you loved my AJR H2O energy drink and then we became pretty good friends and I've visited you all over the map since then. You've encouraged me to get into computer science and web development, and that means the world to me because I barely believe in myself!

I cherish you and I want you to know our memories together hold a special place in my heart. You're included in the collective experiences that make me who I am today, and I am forever grateful.

— Austin Robinson

Send   Cancel

Sunday, November 22nd, 11:44

Varun Cross,

If you're reading this, it's because you 'liked' a Facebook post I made back in 2018. I know it's been awhile, but I'm happy to present your very own webpage and my favorite memory with you!

My favorite memory with you is when you wore Crocs that one time. I know that's incredibly vague, but I think that's when I realized I actually do like Crocs. You converted me. Also, I genuinely love your smile and how happy you are all the time. Remember that one time you were Santa in front of Gregory Gym at UT Austin because of that Texas Blazers event? Miss that!

I cherish you and I want you to know our memories together hold a special place in my heart. You're included in the collective experiences that make me who I am today, and I am forever grateful.

— Austin Robinson

Send　　**Cancel**

Sunday, November 22nd, 11:47

Will Webster,

If you're reading this, it's because you 'liked' a Facebook post I made back in 2018. I know it's been awhile, but I'm happy to present your very own webpage and my favorite memory with you!

My favorite memory with you - and one of my favorites in my whole life - is sitting on my bed with you and watching the new Degrassi season. I cannot remember for the life of me why we even did that. But it was so nice and all we wanted to do was hang out with each other and not have to think about our personal lives. I wish I could do that with you again!

I cherish you and I want you to know our memories together hold a special place in my heart. You're included in the collective experiences that make me who I am today, and I am forever grateful.

— Austin Robinson

 Send **Cancel**

Sunday, November 22nd, 11:48

Yasmeen Tate,

If you're reading this, it's because you 'liked' a Facebook post I made back in 2018. I know it's been awhile, but I'm happy to present your very own webpage and my favorite memory with you!

OMG, I have not heard from you in so, so long. Like, 2013 long. We went to HOBY's Advanced Leadership Academy together, which is a special bond because they basically shut it down after a couple more. Thank you for experiencing that unique conference with me and making that time one of my favorites in life. I hope you're doing well and doing your best!

I cherish you and I want you to know our memories together hold a special place in my heart. You're included in the collective experiences that make me who I am today, and I am forever grateful.

— Austin Robinson

Send   Cancel

Sunday, November 22nd, 11:53

Zach Lindsey,

If you're reading this, it's because you 'liked' a Facebook post I made back in 2018. I know it's been awhile, but I'm happy to present your very own webpage and my favorite memory with you!

My favorite memory with you is having fun with you at literally any and every Alpha Phi Omega event. We basically both threw our lives into APO, so we saw each other A LOT. Me, you, Zachary, and a whole lot of other people knew each other so well during our university career. I miss that time and I could only be so lucky to experience comradery like that again!

I cherish you and I want you to know our memories together hold a special place in my heart. You're included in the collective experiences that make me who I am today, and I am forever grateful.

— Austin Robinson

 Send   **Cancel**

Zachary Lyons,

If you're reading this, it's because you 'liked' a Facebook post I made back in 2018. I know it's been awhile, but I'm happy to present your very own webpage and my favorite memory with you!

My favorite memory with you is when we met on Twitter & Instagram back in October of 2018 and immediately clicked. We had such an intense relationship for that month, and now we are the best of friends. Kind of like 'Cool' by Gwen Stefani, but also not at all! I know you're finding your place in Nova Scotia, and I hope you end up doing something you love!

I cherish you and I want you to know our memories together hold a special place in my heart. You're included in the collective experiences that make me who I am today, and I am forever grateful.

— Austin Robinson

Send   **Cancel**

Sunday, November 22nd, 11:57

Zack Parsons,

If you're reading this, it's because you 'liked' a Facebook post I made back in 2018. I know it's been awhile, but I'm happy to present your very own webpage and my favorite memory with you!

My favorite memory with you is when I spent the night at your condo in Austin, Texas and watched you play Legend of Zelda: Breathe of the Wild on my Nintendo Switch. And then I just let you keep my Switch for, like, six months because you seemed to like it so much and I never got into it! But then I did years later. Anyway, thank you for your continued friendship!

I cherish you and I want you to know our memories together hold a special place in my heart. You're included in the collective experiences that make me who I am today, and I am forever grateful.

– Austin Robinson

Send   **Cancel**

Sunday, November 22nd, 11:59

Zackary Petty,

If you're reading this, it's because you 'liked' a Facebook post I made back in 2018. I know it's been awhile, but I'm happy to present your very own webpage and my favorite memory with you!

My favorite memory with you is when we traveled to Seattle and quite literally immediately got a parking ticket at the Museum of Pop Culture (totally on brand for us). OMG and then we went gay night-club hopping across the city, but it was right when the pandemic started so nothing was fun and we didn't know what we were doing. And we still don't!

I cherish you and I want you to know our memories together hold a special place in my heart. You're included in the collective experiences that make me who I am today, and I am forever grateful.

- Austin Robinson

Send   Cancel

Sunday, November 22nd, 12:01

Zoey Brooks,

If you're reading this, it's because you 'liked' a Facebook post I made back in 2018. I know it's been awhile, but I'm happy to present your very own webpage and my favorite memory with you!

My favorite memory with you is when you and our mutual friend Travis came to visit me in Portland, Oregon and we went to the Multnomah County Whiskey Library and got totally drunk. You didn't read the price on the menu and accidentally bought a $60 drink, so we just went along with it, LOL. Actually, my favorite memory with you is that ENTIRE trip!

I cherish you and I want you to know our memories together hold a special place in my heart. You're included in the collective experiences that make me who I am today, and I am forever grateful.

– Austin Robinson

Send   Cancel

Sunday, November 22nd, 12:04

Zane Simons,

If you're reading this, it's because you 'liked' a Facebook post I made back in 2018. I know it's been awhile, but I'm happy to present your very own webpage and my favorite memory with you!

My favorite memory with you is when you bought a couple Madagascar Hissing Cockroaches and they basically immediately started breeding. Within a month's time, you had dozens of cockroaches and not even the local zoos, animal shops, and bug enthusiasts would take them off of your hands. You also made me make a remix of 'This Kiss' by Faith Hill that said, "This Hiss." Anyway!

I cherish you and I want you to know our memories together hold a special place in my heart. You're included in the collective experiences that make me who I am today, and I am forever grateful.

— Austin Robinson

Send   **Cancel**

Sunday, November 22nd, 12:06

Zara Wallace,

If you're reading this, it's because you 'liked' a Facebook post I made back in 2018. I know it's been awhile, but I'm happy to present your very own webpage and my favorite memory with you!

My favorite memory with you is when we bought matching outfits together just to take a pandemic picture of us high-fiving virtually. It did kind of look like we were in the same place physically high-fiving! I am so excited to see you crush the MCAT, go onto Med School, and become the best Pediatrician ever. I have no doubt that you will achieve everything you want!

I cherish you and I want you to know our memories together hold a special place in my heart. You're included in the collective experiences that make me who I am today, and I am forever grateful.

– Austin Robinson

Send   Cancel

Sunday, November 22nd, 12:09

Zander Lights,

If you're reading this, it's because you 'liked' a Facebook post I made back in 2018. I know it's been awhile, but I'm happy to present your very own webpage and my favorite memory with you!

My favorite memory with you is when we visited my hometown and they were serendipitously having a wine event across the entirety of downtown. And later that night, you contracted the norovirus, which you then gave to me a week later! But actually, my favorite memory is all of the ones we've made throughout the past two years. There are way too many to count!

I cherish you and I want you to know our memories together hold a special place in my heart. You're included in the collective experiences that make me who I am today, and I am forever grateful.

— Austin Robinson

Send   **Cancel**

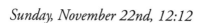

Sunday, November 22nd, 12:12

Zephyr Heights,

If you're reading this, it's because you 'liked' a Facebook post I made back in 2018. I know it's been awhile, but I'm happy to present your very own webpage and my favorite memory with you!

My favorite memory with you is when we attended the HOBY Training Institute together (you representing California and me representing Alaska) and made fun of the United States Census, randomly. You were the most fun person there and I have no clue how that conference would have gone without you. You literally make my experiences better!

I cherish you and I want you to know our memories together hold a special place in my heart. You're included in the collective experiences that make me who I am today, and I am forever grateful.

– Austin Robinson

Send   Cancel

Sunday, November 22nd, 12:15

Zahid Zuri,

If you're reading this, it's because you 'liked' a Facebook post I made back in 2018. I know it's been awhile, but I'm happy to present your very own webpage and my favorite memory with you!

You are credited as being an inspiration of mine at the beginning of this book! Although someone else inspired me to get into graphic design, you are my continued supporter and you teach me more than I could ever ask for. Thank you for allowing me to use your name on our collaborative books and being one of the funniest humans I know!

I cherish you and I want you to know our memories together hold a special place in my heart. You're included in the collective experiences that make me who I am today, and I am forever grateful.

– Austin Robinson

 Send **Cancel** 188

Sunday, November 22nd, 12:17

Zola Parker,

If you're reading this, it's because you 'liked' a Facebook post I made back in 2018. I know it's been awhile, but I'm happy to present your very own webpage and my favorite memory with you!

My favorite memory with you - aside from getting married to you as a joke - is when I visited you in Salt Lake City, Utah and got some great biscuits and gravy that we ate in the park. You have been there for me ever since we met back in university and I cannot wait to see where your life takes you. I'm always here if you ever need anything, and you know that!

I cherish you and I want you to know our memories together hold a special place in my heart. You're included in the collective experiences that make me who I am today, and I am forever grateful.

— Austin Robinson

Send   Cancel

Z

So what did I learn this time around? Maybe 2.5 years is an appropriate amount of time between Friendship Project novels! If I were to conduct and write one of these every single year, that would be A LOT of unpaid time spent. Don't get me wrong - these projects are fun to make, they increase my skillset, and I don't expect to capitalize off of friendship. However, it would still be 100+ hours a year that I could spend changing my life in some other meaningful way. Or 100+ hours a year I could be volunteering to change the lives of underprivileged populations.

In fact, between 2018 and now, I learned that I can conduct Friendship Projects in a less time-consuming way that will reach more people. For example, in August of 2018, I set out to send as many people as possible a unique selfie of me waving at them via Twitter. Over 500 people participated. In December of 2018, I asked my Twitter followers if I could put their usernames as ornaments on my Christmas Tree - over 1,000 people ended up on my tree. In January of 2019, I created a New Years Resolution website (www.2020re.solutions) where I asked people to be my pen pal for the purposes of keeping them accountable for their goals - 250 people realized their potential. Again in January of 2019, I announced I was writing a book and that I had several extra pages to fill; I offered my Twitter followers a shout-out. Over 2,000 people now live at the end of my book 'The Sea Section' (2019).

Those stunts may sound like they took a long time - and they did - but they took a significantly less amount of time than 'Project Letters' and 'Project Webpages'. And I reached almost 10x the amount of people. Granted, most of the people on Twitter are internet strangers - but that doesn't lessen my admiration for them or their gratitude for being included in a Friendship Project. In fact, I gained over 10,000 followers in just four months because these projects really struck a chord with people. Before, I was just trying to make my friends smile, and then I learned I can instill a little happiness in online communities where the impact and impressions have larger boundaries.

But this book is about the real friends in my real life. So more importantly, I assessed and evaluated my friendship with 180 people - people I have known from childhood to just a couple years ago. I expressed my appreciation for them not only to myself throughout this process, but also through these webpages. I gained a deeper understanding of what friendship means to me and what each and every one of these friends has contributed to that understanding. My passion for treating the people in my life as celebrities has only deepened and rooted itself in my actions.

The purpose of turning this project into a novel is to document my appreciation for my friends, and let it be known that I care for them and am willing to go out of my way to ensure they feel valued. I can spread this activity to others and hope for a movement where we treasure the people in our lives and actively think about friendship opposed to simply allowing it to be a passive act in our lives.

More specifically, I learned that I have friends from all over the world. I made these webpages for people from several different countries, backgrounds, and lifestyles. I was surprised to learn that my friends are widely spread out and have experiences vastly different than my own. I began to appreciate those differences, because they allow me to access a worldview that I wouldn't have otherwise. Although I do enjoy when me and a friend are similar and can relate on a variety of levels, I believe it is important to not only befriend those who come from backgrounds that are uncomfortable to us, but also utilize their experience and knowledge to help yourself grow as a human being. And that's not a one-way street - I can guarantee that if you are growing due to someone's understanding of life, then they are also growing from yours. Lessons learned don't always have to be intrapersonal - they can be interpersonal, too. Or better yet, they can be expressed via webpages of appreciation. Also, I have way too many friends with the same name as me.

And finally, I learned that I have some kick-ass friends. They have done incredible things, from building their own companies to working for prominent politicians to making art in Chicago, and then some. They have traveled the world, started families, and written the foreword to this book. They perform in drag, drive the Oscar Meyer Weinermobile, and speak five different languages. My friends have had intense and life-changing experiences that I may not completely understand, but can learn from simply by calling them my friend.

I'm not sure what the future of my Friendship Projects looks like, but I will never stop ensuring my friends understand how much they matter in the lives of their friends and loved ones.

NOW IT'S YOUR TURN

So, here's your homework. I want you to do as I did and create webpages for over 180 people. I'm kidding - I want you to simply write a "webpage" for at least one person regarding what you appreciate about them. You can do this in two different ways: 1). Head over to my GitHub page (github.com/ausitnjamesrobinson) and download my 'ProjectWebpages' code, or 2). On the next page, I have included six templates for you. If you're reading this on a computer, screenshot the templates and go wild. If you're holding a physical book, rip out the following pages and mail them. You could fill them out and then mail the entire book to a person's physical location for all I care. Just tell your friends and your loved ones how much you appreciate them.

Date: *Time:*

_____,

_____

_____

_____

1). _____

_____

_____

_____

_____

2). _____

_____

_____

_____

_____

3). _____

_____

_____

_____

_____

\- _____

Send   Cancel

Date: _____   *Time:* _____

_____,

    _____

_____

_____

1). _____

_____

_____

_____

_____

2). _____

_____

_____

_____

_____

3). _____

_____

_____

_____

_____

                    — _____

Send   Cancel

Date: *Time:*

_____,

_____

_____

_____

1). _____

_____

_____

_____

_____

2). _____

_____

_____

_____

_____

3). _____

_____

_____

_____

_____

      - _____

Date: _____ *Time:* _____

_____,

_____

_____

_____

1). _____

_____

_____

_____

_____

2). _____

_____

_____

_____

_____

3). _____

_____

_____

_____

_____

- _____

Send   **Cancel**

Date: *Time:*

_____,

_____
_____
_____

1). _____
_____
_____
_____
_____

2). _____
_____
_____
_____
_____

3). _____
_____
_____
_____
_____

\- _____

Send   **Cancel**

Date: _____ Time: _____

_____ ,

_____

_____

_____

1). _____

_____

_____

_____

2). _____

_____

_____

_____

3). _____

_____

_____

_____

_____

— _____

Send   **Cancel**

THE TOOLS

I want to provide you with the tools I used to make this project a reality. I'm not asking that you write your own book on friendship (feel free to though), but maybe this will inspire someone else in some kind of way. Plus, I love sharing how I conduct and complete my projects.

Concept

For the concept, I used Facebook to find participants, as you saw at the beginning of the book, and to keep in communication with them. I used Microsoft Word as a way to track each person who 'liked' the post. I also consulted my previous book 'Project Letters'.

Book

When it comes to the physical book, I used Adobe InDesign to format and write the pages. This was my first time using InDesign as opposed to Microsoft Word to accomplish this! For the cover, I used a dimensions template by KDP Publishing and InDesign to design it - or really adapt it from Christopher Sullivan's original design. To sign off on each Webpage, I created my own font based on my handwriting thanks to Calligraphr's easy typeface template. The original AJR Publications company logo comes from the mind of Christopher Sullivan via Adobe Illustrator. The layout of the Webpages was designed in InDesign and inspired by the book 'TTYL' (2004) by Lauren Myracle. Finally, I used Facebook to look up the participants I gathered in 2018, and for memories.

Website

To create the website, I moved away from using WIX and decided to code it myself. I've been learning how to code, so this was really exciting for me. I used HTML and CSS in Visual Studio Code, which I pushed to GitHub with Git via the Hyper terminal. I used InDesign to design the homepage, the name cards that you see after the homepage, and the webpages connected to the name cards. For color, I used the RGB color model, with a difference in five values between colors, for the name cards and webpage designs. I used Vercel to host my GitHub repository and deploy the site: https://www.projectweb.page

Publishing

Self-publishing is SO easy and cheap nowadays, but sometimes I worry that the people in my life think I keep getting book deals from major publishers. So I'll tell you my process for publishing! For this book, I'm going to use KDP Publishing to upload the cover, document, and details for Print-On-Demand (POD) purposes.

(Sometimes I use Lulu, but only for pocket-sized books). I'll also upload the cover and details over at Bowker, the U.S. ISBN website used to locate books - this is also where I got the barcode for this book! Once approved by both services, 'Project Webpages' is officially good to go and will be up on every major distribution site (e.g. Amazon, Barnes & Nobel, etc.).

Marketing

Marketing is not necessarily my forte, and I don't know the proper tools to utilize it to its fullest extent. I'll use Instagram and Facebook to market the book, as most people would. I've already designed the social media posts via InDesign. As I said under publishing, the book will be available through all major distribution sites. Book stores and libraries also have the chance to pick it up, but typically a book requires a lot of traction before those establishments would carry it.

On the next several pages are many of the tools and outcomes mentioned in this section!

the

austin

james

robinson

font

color spectrum

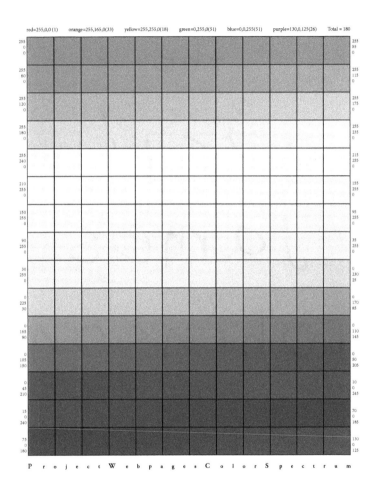

homepage

name cards

Aaron Smith

Chris Anderson

Kurt Kelly

Olivia Carroll

Stewart Bowman

Yasmeen Tate

Zola Parker

logos

AJR
PUB
LICATIONS

website: www.projectweb.page

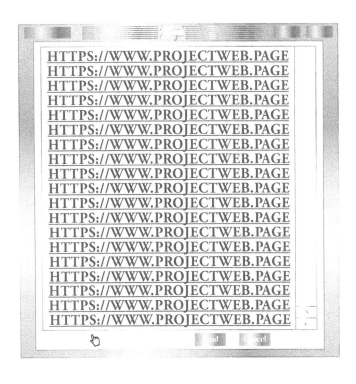

prequel: <u>Project Letters</u>

Project Letters

**A Collection of 215 Letters
to People I May or May Not Know**

Austin James Robinson & Co.

ABOUT THE AUTHOR

www.austinjamesrobinson.com